A QUICK DRINK

THE
SPEED RACK GUIDE to
Winning Cocktails
FOR ANY MOOD

BY **LYNNETTE MARRERO** AND **IVY MIX**
WITH **MEGAN KRIGBAUM**

CONTENTS

Jess Pomerantz up in lights as the national winner in Speed Rack Season 10.

INTRODUCTION

—●●●•

IF YOU CLOSE YOUR EYES AND LISTEN,

you could be at any sporting event anywhere in the world: spectators chanting and cheering, a commentator giving the play-by-play, each competitor's sighs, gasps, and hurrahs, everyone's eyes on the clock.

It's 2016, the national finals of Speed Rack Season 5, and it's come down to Julia Gordon, a bartender from Chicago with a sweet smile, tortoise-shell glasses, gold chains, and a ponytail that's been garnished with flowers. It's her first time at Nationals. Her opponent is Lacy Hawkins, originally a competitor in Portland, Oregon, and then in New York City, with a pink, side-shaved bob, wide-gauge ear plugs, and the confidence of someone who's done this before—it's her fifth season competing, and she is cool and calm in her thirst for the win. Two years before, in her final round, tragedy struck at the last moment when she went to hit the buzzer on her bar and the force toppled drinks, bottles, and mixing glasses everywhere. There's a lot riding on this.

As at the start of each round, Julia and Lacy place their right hands on their big red buzzers, left hands in the air, and the host, Chris Patino, wearing a pink suit covered in Speed Rack logos, counts down with the audience, "Five! Four! Three! Two! One! GOOOOOO!"

This is the grand finale, the Dealer's Choice round, and the judges have made their requests: an original low-ABV cocktail for Julie Reiner, bartender and owner of Brooklyn's Clover Club; a classic Sazerac for cocktail historian David Wondrich; a Last Word for Kate Krader, then the restaurant editor of *Food & Wine* magazine, and a swizzle-style tropical drink for Paul McGee, who at the time was the bartender and owner of Chicago's Lost Lake.

Julia and Lacy have had fifteen minutes to wrap their brains around these prompts and set up their bar as needed. And then it's off to the races. They move efficiently and fast. Julia dashes bitters, Lacy begins filling a mixing glass with ice. Julia is shaking with one arm, stirring with the other. Lacy is stirring and straw-tasting along the way. At one point Lacy dashes absinthe into a rocks glass and tosses it into the air, coating the insides of the glass with true flair.

"Sazerac!" she shouts. The crowd loses its collective mind—the esteemed judges do, too.

The two pour their drinks, almost in sync. Garnishes are placed in glasses. Lacy surveys the drinks in front of her and slams her buzzer to stop the timer; seconds later, Julia follows suit.

"Julia, I asked for something original, but this drink is pretty close to a classic Bamboo," says Julie. "I was hoping for something a little more creative." Julia gets a five-second penalty. Lacy's drink—an inverted Manhattan with two parts sherry to one part rye (a recipe passed down by fellow competitor Karen Grill)—gets more love. "Lacy, this is beautiful and has so much depth. I gave you plus zero." Perfect score!

Next to be judged are the Sazeracs, both of which Dave, still grinning about Lacy's theatrics, finds to be without flaw. The room becomes increasingly antsy and shockingly quiet.

"I'm so impressed by everybody who competed today, but you two took it to a completely different level," says Paul.

In the end, Chris takes center stage to announce the final scores. "Julia Gordon's final time, with penalties, is two minutes and fifty-five seconds. Lacy Hawkins's final time . . ." The host pauses to take a deep breath. "Two minutes and fifty-two seconds." You can barely hear what he says next: "It's been five years in the making, but the winner of Season 5 of Speed Rack is Lacy Hawkins!"

Cue the Champagne showers. Lacy finds redemption. Finally.

———•——•—

And this is how it's been for about thirteen years now. We've been traveling around the country and the world, exalting the women bartenders who are relentless—proving that they are not only very much in the game—they are, in fact, *creating* the game.

We are Lynnette Marrero and Ivy Mix, co-founders of Speed Rack and women who've made bartending our lifelong careers. That might not sound all that remarkable today, but when we first launched Speed Rack in New York City, we were considered anomalies in the bar world.

We were keenly aware when we'd travel to the best bars around the globe that there weren't a whole lot of women bartending in them. If you wanted to get a good cocktail at the time, in the mid-to-late aughts, you were mostly going to a speakeasy, where everyone was hearkening back to Prohibition and personifying the Jerry Thomases of the world, with vests and armbands and mustaches, to boot.

We first met one night at Mayahuel, an East Village cocktail bar, in 2009. Ivy worked there and Lynnette was doing a favor, pinch-hitting as a cocktail server for the night. We very quickly recognized a similarity in our work ethic, helping each other run drinks and just getting the job done.

It was over chicken wings and cheap beers while watching the Super Bowl in 2011 that Ivy started talking with Lynnette about her idea for an all-women competition to promote the incredible bartenders that weren't getting the attention—or the jobs—that they deserved. Lynnette was exactly the person she needed as a partner.

By this point Lynnette had already begun to find her own community of professional bartending women in New York, having worked at Julie Reiner's groundbreaking Flatiron Lounge with Katie Stipe, as well as at Freemans with bartender Yana Volfson. In 2008, Lynnette founded the New York City chapter of LUPEC (Ladies United for the Preservation of Endangered Cocktails)—a networking group for women. She started the organization after first being bartender Flynn Mchee at Louis 649 on the Lower East Side and realizing that there were more outstanding women bartenders in her own city she

Marisela Dobson suits up for her round in New Orleans, Season 11.

Friends and fans gather around Jess Pomerantz after her win.

had not yet met. After a trip to New Orleans later that summer, Lynnette met Misty Kalkofen and Kitty Amann from LUPEC's Boston chapter and decided to launch the New York City group. Following Boston's lead, the NYC organization focused on executing fundraising events for predominantly women's-based charity organizations but also to raise funds for hospitality crisis causes. The idea was to set up guest bartender nights at bars around town, highlighting the women talent, sponsored by brands, particularly women-founded or -led spirits companies.

In those days, we'd talk with bar managers and owners and say, "So, why don't you have any women bartenders?" and the response was almost always the same, "Oh, I don't know any." Speed Rack was founded as a direct response to this daft assertion.

Ivy's concept for Speed Rack was to elevate women in the industry by putting them on a stage so that there was no hunt required, and, as a bonus, prove to these bartenders that this work could be a sustainable career. It was our way of saying, "There's your platform; go stand on it and jump up and down and be SEEN." We'd give them a chance to show off the skills they used every night behind the bar. We'd get sponsors and donate all the money to breast cancer charities.

With Lynnette's network and experience in philanthropy and Ivy's strong competitive edge, we started talking about it with everyone we knew and, not six months later, we were hosting our first Speed Rack event—a whirling Roller Derby with a nod to Rosie the Riveter, flashes of hot pink, and undeniable unstoppability.

———•—•

Something that becomes ever more evident as the years go by is that there's a reason bartending was for so long a man's sport—it is frustratingly unsustainable for the long haul, even more so for women who want to have children. For the most part, there's no such thing as health insurance or maternity leave in this field. It's a big reason that we have watched as many in our network (including those who have no interest in having children!) take on jobs that pull them out from behind the bar into brand positions and on corporate ladders that come with a certain level of security. These sorts of jobs are evidence of an unavoidable evolution of our industry. And at the same time we cheer on those breaking glass ceilings, we do feel some sadness that so many women have stopped bartending in order to do so. It is our hope that this industry that we love will catch up and empower more of us to stay doing the work we do so well.

We follow in the footsteps of the undeniable all-star bartenders, who have been our mentors and our beacons, including Bridget Albert, Misty Kalkofen, Julie Reiner, and Audrey Saunders. These women have more than carved out space; they have led by extraordinary example and impacted the drinking culture in their cities, the US, and the world.

In 2019, we were honored with two awards at Tales of the Cocktail (an important industry foundation): the Philanthropy Award and World's Best Bar Mentor. These honors get to exactly what we are seeking to do with Speed Rack: to pay forward the mentorship that we have received—from our peers, predecessors, and the next generation—and to give as generously and as abundantly as we can.

ABOUT THIS BOOK

———•••——

FOR MORE THAN A DECADE WE HAVE HAD THE GREAT LUCK TO WITNESS HUNDREDS OF BADASS WOMEN BARTENDERS ACROSS THE WORLD MAKING DRINKS.

There isn't one Speed Rack round that goes by where we don't pick up something new—a technique, a flavor combination, an improved eyeliner cat eye, or a new friend or twenty. These women are defining the bar world with a style all their own. And we wanted to give this talent an even bigger stage than our competitions, in the form of a book that can be read anywhere, even if you have not experienced Speed Rack firsthand. We want to celebrate the women who make our industry great, while helping everyone make better drinks more intuitively. With this book, we are sharing our incredible brain trust with you. There's something in these pages for both the home bartender who's never stirred martini, as well as the professional ones who could do it in their sleep.

ABOUT THE RECIPES

———•——

The cocktails here are inspired by the Dealer's Choice round in the finals of every Speed Rack competition (see page 16). This challenge is not only meant to showcase a competitor's ability to work quickly and efficiently behind the bar, but also their skills in improvising a drink for a guest based on something other than a standard drink order—be it a mood, an occasion, an emotion, an open-ended idea. It's how we most often decide what to drink, right? How we're feeling, what the weather's like, who we're drinking with, and why—all play a role in what we'll choose.

To empower you not only when sitting at the bar, but also standing behind it, we've gone to dozens of bartenders in our community with brand-new, made-for-this-book dealer's choice prompts, similar to those that come into play during the competition. These prompts have been specifically created to suggest moods and styles of cocktail. Maybe you don't know that you want a cantaloupe wine spritzer, but you do know that you want something fruity, fizzy, and a little bitter. Maybe you're on a bar crawl with friends and want something low-proof but don't want to spend time reading through a drinks list. Maybe you just want to curl up on the couch with a book and a mug full of . . . something.

The 101 recipes that we share with you here are their answers to our call, and offer up exceptional drinks, tailored for a multitude of preferences. Consider these recipes pathways and their methods and ideologies inspiration.

During the competition, the opportunity for making a spiced pineapple syrup, jalapeño-infused tequila, or black pepper tincture doesn't exist (it is a *speed* competition, after all). But offstage, Speed Rack competitors are behind the best bars in the world—and they're certainly making syrups and shrubs and made-to-order sparkling coconut water. Many of the cocktails in this book are simple as can be, while others involve some real prep (or glitter). All are a unique representation of the impressive talent that has kept Speed Rack going for over a decade.

You'll find some of our own recipes included here, too (they're labeled "From the Founders"). These are drinks that we have perfected over the years and we have zeroed in on the sorts of drinkers that will take pleasure in them.

Also in the mix are "Modern Classics," cocktails from well-established women bartenders who have become legendary in our industry—they're drinks that have found a following across the world and have seen numerous iterations in a short time span. Whereas "classic" cocktails are the OG, these drinks are the *new guard*, and define our drinking and bar culture today in a matter of sips. Their creators are our mentors and friends.

This book is organized into eight chapters (from lighter to boozier) by drink style. Within each, you'll find a variety of spirits and methods intermixed, with the understanding that some drinkers will want a brisk and bitter drink when celebrating, while others might be looking for something fruity in their coupe; for some a vacation drink might resemble a piña colada, whereas the person at the bar next to you is expecting an old-fashioned. There's plenty of room for invention once you have a sense of intention.

ABOUT THE COMMUNITY

—•—•—

Dashed in throughout these pages are tips to help you improve your game, as well as notes from competitors and members of the Speed Rack community to give you a feel for this incredible network.

And finally, as we'll say many times throughout this book, Speed Rack is, at its heart, a classic cocktail competition. The only way to win is to know the classics (and the modern classics!) cold. These drinks are proven reliable templates that can be used to create new drinks, whether you're a novice or a pro. While we know not everyone will be making flashcards and memorizing ratios, they are the perfect jumping off points. You'll find our must-know specs in the back of this book, beginning on page 254. Get practicing and then practice some more.

Back the Rack.

A WORD ABOUT "WOMEN"

Throughout this book, you'll notice we refer to Speed Rack competitors and friends as "women," a term that is inclusive of anyone who identifies as such. As language continues to evolve, we recognize that it's likely this word might not fully encapsulate the diversity of gender expression experienced by everyone included here, but we hope to be part of this ongoing conversation and will continue to welcome all who want to be part of our community.

WHAT IS SPEED RACK?

Speed Rack is a great many things to a great many people, but at its very core, it is a classic cocktail speed competition for the fiercest women bartenders around the world. Speed Rack creates a stage for these professional bartenders to show off their skills and advance in their careers.

More than a feminist platform, we are also an organization that, since the very beginning, has raised funds for breast cancer research, awareness, and education. Thanks to our sponsors, we are able to donate 100 percent of the proceeds from our events to those vetted charities that fit our ethos. Even a portion of proceeds from this book will go to such organizations. For further details about our commitment to breast cancer charities, see Back the Rack, page 53.

Speed Rack, as an organization, is a massive network with thousands of bartenders competing over the course of the last thirteen years. This group of competitors and volunteers is so tight, we'll often hear on a competition day, "Happy Speed Rack!" as if it's an industry holiday.

And for many, Speed Rack is a family. We have witnessed so many beautiful and important connections and alliances made over the years, be it through mentorships, helping someone find a job, or elevating the diverse talent pool within the bar community. It's an opportunity to empower those who face discrimination in a completely accepting, nurturing, and encouraging way.

Over the years we have hosted various initiatives, such as the Sisterhood Project, which began as a series of talks and chats related to issues within the industry—from health and wellness to accounting to sexual harassment. Over the last few years, this project has been absorbed into Speed Rack itself with mentorship, access, and education as top priorities. During the pandemic in 2020, when we could not do live events, we launched a very intentional program where we paired professionals at the top of their game with young, budding talent around the world. At times, Speed Rack functions as a job fair with bar owners and brand recruiters joining the crowd with an eye toward recruiting new talent. We love watching this happen. It's exactly why we created the competition in the first place—to prove that not only were there great women bartenders everywhere, but that they deserved the spotlight. Looking for some incredible talent to run the show? Here they are!

Speed Rack is also importantly and emphatically a disco ball–spinning, hot pink explosion of cocktails and feminism. It's a tattoos flaunting, strong arms–shaking, no-holds-barred party with DJs dropping the hits and bucketfuls of punch from our sponsors.

HOW SPEED RACK WORKS

———•——•———

With each season of Speed Rack, we draw up a list of cities we want to hit that year—regions around the country—and the world—where we'll host competitions. In the United States, we've had up to twelve regional competitions in a single season, all leading up to the national finals. In other countries and continents, which have included Canada, Mexico, the UK, Asia, Puerto Rico, and Australia, we'll have one national or regional contest. We have unparalleled coordinators, collaborators, and volunteers in every city who help us pull this off. It takes a village!

And then the recruiting begins. In the first few years, we had to really work to get the word out, using our local networks and various chapters of LUPEC (Ladies United for the Preservation of Endangered Cocktails) to not only give the competition credibility, but also help find competitors. From the start, we've been producing videos so that curious bartenders could get a sense of what the competition was all about. And over the years, our Speed Rack alums have become our greatest ambassadors, bringing up the next generation of bartenders and then sending them our way. Having done this for over a decade now, we might have 120 applicants for a single event—when we're only looking for about 20 to 25.

Every prospective competitor submits a written application where we ask a slew of questions covering everything from "how do you work for diversity in the workplace?" to "has breast cancer affected someone you love?" to "who do you look up to in this industry?" to "what's your favorite guilty pleasure drink?" Some applicants even submit videos. And then we start reading. We are looking for professional bartenders, with incredible drive and passion for the craft, who are also in search of community. It's usually a range from absolute pros to newbies and everyone in between, which we've seen foster growth in every direction.

After we make our selections, we send the chosen competitors a "spec book" of more than sixty cocktail recipes that we expect they'd be able to make at a moment's notice. These drinks will comprise most of the competition. We believe that any bartender worth their margarita salt will have a good grasp on the many classics that paved the way for our industry, the framework for everything else. Before you can make a bespoke cocktail menu, you need the basics—we think of it as learning the fundamentals of drawing before painting a masterpiece.

Once our invite letters are sent, then begins the real training and obsessive practicing. One former winner even went so far as to construct a bar in her bedroom so that she could practice as early or as late as she wanted without disturbing roommates.

Speed Rack day begins with a prelims round. Prelims are basically torture—just one competitor in a room with four judges, a bar, and a whole lot of anxiety. We'll give them four drinks to make (from a list of six they'd been alerted to in their acceptance letter), start the clock, and stand back. Here, free pouring (without measuring in jiggers) tends to be the name of the game. It's a flurry of daring multi-bottle pours, quick two-hand shakes, and

CLOCKWISE FROM TOP LEFT: Chicago always shows up; judges Christine Wiseman, Earlecia Richelle, and Meaghan Dorman await a round of drinks in NYC in Season 11; Marina Holter pours one out in New Orleans in Season 10; Ivy serves up a couple of Cosmopolitans in the Midwest competition in Season 11; judge Vance Henderson considers a couple of tropical drinks in Season 10; Fabiola Juarez came with a crew; a Lynnette and Elyse Blechman lovefest in New Orleans in Season 10.

loudly clinking ice. Over the last decade we have seen this round get faster and faster. In order to get onstage these days, competitors need to be able to execute the four drinks in under 75 seconds. It's lightning fast.

When it comes to judging prelims, it's a little like ordering a margarita in a club; you know it's gonna be in a plastic cup over crummy ice, but it will be in your hand fast. The expectations are slightly lower; what we care most about in this round is speed, but our judges still assess the drinks in several categories including balance, conformity, correct glassware, and washline (the fill level of the drink)—and will assign time penalties as necessary. The eight fastest competitors make it to the stage that evening before hundreds of people—friends, fans, family, and a whole lot of industry folks.

The sound is unbelievable with the crowd cheering and waving posters. The lights are hot, the ice is melting, and the cameras are in your face. It's nothing like working in a cocktail bar and yet, that's exactly where you are. These rounds work on a bracketed system just like March Madness or the World Cup. In the quarterfinals, the fastest goes up against the eighth fastest, the second fastest against the seventh, and so on.

The quarterfinals and semifinals are all about the classics, with each judge ordering up whatever fits their fancy. In these rounds, each competitor has a barback, as they would on any insane Saturday night at a packed bar. This person helps with organization, grabbing bottles, and whatever else falls in the mania of the round, and providing the most important thing: moral support.

Here, the judges (industry titans, writers, and chefs) are much more serious about precision than in prelims, considering balance, dilution, garnish, with time penalties (in .5-second increments) applied for any mishaps at their discretion. "Too watered down!" "Wish you'd put more sugar in there." "Would have liked to have had a garnish!" "What the hell is in this glass?" Zero seconds tacked on means you made the perfect drink, but penalties can go all the way to 30 seconds, in which case, something is seriously amiss.

At long last, it's the final competition, with just two bartenders left and so much at stake. It's time for the Dealer's Choice round.

DEALER'S CHOICE

———•———

Dealer's Choice is different from the rest of the rounds in Speed Rack in that it's the only one that's not strictly tied to the classics, though most bartenders will use them as a springboard for their innovations. This is where we get to see competitors add their own special sauce to what they're doing behind the bar—improvising from clues dropped by their judges.

This round is inspired by the more freewheeling version of bartending you have likely witnessed at many a craft cocktail bar—where an off-menu concoction is devised on the spot to suit the whims of the customer. We set up the scene like this: It's a busy Saturday night and you're positively slammed. You look up and who's walking through the door, but four cocktail luminaries: Dale DeGroff, Julie Reiner, Dave Wondrich, and Audrey Saunders. These are the people who made the category. They've run legendary bars, written definitive books; they've shaken, they've stirred, and they know their way behind the stick. They sit down at your bar and don't even look at the menu you've worked on tirelessly, instead they all its, "I'd like a tropical old-fashioned," "Make me a Clover Club (you know it's Julie's signature drink), "Give me a low ABV sherry cocktail, up," "I was in Venice last

week and I miss it already; can I have something that will take me back?" And there you are. You have no choice but to whip up four flawlessly executed drinks—as fast as you can so you can get back to all the other people piling up at the bar. What do you do?

You set up your glasses in front of you, grab your shaker and your mixing glass, and get to work. You've done this before. This is your chance to flex your skills and your creativity—to give them what they want, without them knowing exactly what that is.

In the Dealer's Choice round at Speed Rack, each judge orders a drink, giving their prompt, and the two finalists not only have to come up with the ideal cocktail on the spot, but do so faster and far better than their competitor—all without knocking everything over as they go to hit the buzzer.

As in every round, the drinks are presented to the judges and they taste and consider and give their opinions, adding 5- to 30-second penalties as they see fit—maybe there's not enough bitters, the drink's not quite cold enough, ice chips made it through the strainer, maybe the drink didn't answer the request, maybe it did. True success means there are no penalties at all.

All of these numbers are added up and the evening's host stands between the finalists holding their hands. The room goes quiet in anticipation, people doing arithmetic in their heads to see which competitor in the end comes out on top.

And in a flash, the host announces the winner, holding their arm triumphantly into the air. The victor is hoisted onto the shoulders of barbacks; champagne sprays everywhere. The crowd goes berserk.

And so it goes in every region. We follow this whirlwind format, naming regional winners who will go on to Nationals to do it all over again. There, finally, we celebrate that season's Speed Rack champion.

ABOVE: Katie Renshaw builds her final "dealer's choice" round in Chicago in Season 6.

Shannon Pilz demonstrates the art of the free pour in prelims in the Midwest competition, Season 11.

QUICK TIPS FOR MAKING
A BETTER DRINK

THE BASICS

——●——

We could write a whole book on the intricacies of cocktail making, but frankly, plenty have done that before us, and we'd rather let our Speed Rackers show you their stuff. Here are some baseline concepts to know when using this book:

CHILLED GLASSWARE

The best-case scenario in making drinks is that your serving glass is already cold when you pour a drink into it, preserving all of your efforts in shaking or stirring in a deep chill. This is especially true for drinks that you're planning to serve up—keep your glasses in the freezer while you mix so they're frosty cold. If you don't have enough freezer space (who does, really?) just add a couple of cubes to the glass with a splash of water to get a chill going while you're shaking or stirring, then dump them just before you're ready to fill the glass.

USE FRESH JUICE

You should always mix with fresh juice! Every drink in this book that calls for juice of any sort—pineapple, grapefruit, lemon, lime—is meant to be made with just-squeezed or just-pressed juice, unless otherwise noted. For fruits like pineapple, watermelon, etc., if you don't have a juicer at home, a stop at the local juice bar is a good solution. Otherwise, puree the fruit in a blender and strain out the pulp.

TASTE AND TASTE AGAIN

At every Speed Rack event, Ivy sounds like a broken record telling the competitors to taste all of their ingredients; this is a crucial step in drink making. Not all gins have the same flavor profile, not all grapefruit soda is equally sweet or dry, some ginger syrups are fiery hot, some more sweet and dull, and juices taste different everywhere. (And we mean *everywhere*. We've tried them. Depending on the time of year, citrus juice might be sweeter/more bitter/ more acidic than you're used to.) No matter what you are making, taste and taste and taste and realize you may need to adjust your drinks to accommodate the variance of it all.

GARNISHES

In Speed Rack, we tend not to go too crazy with garnishes—there's neither space nor time—but we do love a beautifully cut citrus twist or a perfect, homemade cocktail onion in a Gibson. When it comes to twists, unless otherwise directed, you'll want to express the citrus oils over the drink, which is to say, hold the twist, peel side down, about 6 inches (15 cm) above the cocktail and give it a little squeeze. This will release all the gorgeous aromatics onto the surface. (We drink with our noses, too!) Then either place the twist in the glass or discard it as per the directions in the recipe.

ABOUT BITTERS

There are a million different bitters on the market now. You'll definitely want to have Angostura or another aromatic bitters, plus Peychaud's and orange bitters of some sort (we're Regan's fans) in order to be able to make the largest range of classics. Some drinks in this book call for very specific bitters outside of those mentioned above—they're the not-so-secret ingredient that can really make a flavor pop. Keep a few that you like on hand.

The topic of "what constitutes a dash?" is a favorite of bartenders because the speed at which bitters come out of a bottle will vary depending on how full the bottle is. You can get a pretty Japanese bitters bottle from Cocktail Kingdom, which does the job of evenly meting out a "dash." But be forewarned that the dashes from these bottles are tiny! Our friends at Death & Co. have calculated that you'll need about 3 dashes from a Japanese bitters bottle to equal one from the original bottle.

CONSTRUCTING
A COCKTAIL

Brittany Bogdan free pours her base
spirits in Season 11 Midwest.

LIQUID BLUEPRINTS

———•—•

Cocktails fall into three distinct categories, depending on how they're constructed: built, shaken, and stirred. Here's our quick guide to each.

BUILT

For built drinks, your mixing vessel is the very glass you'll serve the drink in. You're literally building the cocktail in the glass. For these, the only tool you'll need is a long barspoon.

SHAKEN

Fire up your biceps! Shaken cocktails are made in, well, cocktail shakers. (We like the two-piece shaking tins.) Drinks made with juice (citrus and beyond) are most often shaken in order to aerate, chill, and dilute a drink by forcefully breaking up ice cubes. In Speed Rack, competitors have to master the art of shaking two drinks at a time. But for novices, we recommend using two hands on one shaker, to keep from coating your kitchen in a sticky daiquiri, say. There are all sorts of shaking styles, but for the purpose of this book, shake as you will. If a recipe says to give a quick or gentle shake, that's your cue to not overdo it, so as to achieve proper dilution. A dry shake is one done without ice cubes, a technique frequently used when frothing an egg white into a cocktail.

STIRRED

Drinks that are made without juice are stirred. (Again, rules are made to be broken. See: Jessica Gonzalez's Hot Lips on page 154.) Stirring is a more meditative way of combining ingredients. The mission to chill and dilute remains the same, but when we are stirring a drink, the goal is to not bring any air into it. Here, we smoothly whir the cubes around in a mixing glass, sort of suggesting that everything get along, rather than demanding it. Shaken drinks are well oxygenated, giving a velvety, rich feel; stirred drinks are silky smooth, finding texture through dilution alone. You can stir a drink in half of a cocktail shaker or in a pint glass or in any vessel, really, but if you're into stirred drinks like martinis and Manhattans, we recommend investing in a mixing glass with straight sides; it will make for even dilution and to be honest, it just looks pretty. You'll know your drink is chilled enough when the glass feels very cold to the touch.

ICE

Bartenders notoriously obsess over ice, for good reason. Modern cocktail bars tend to have several expensive ice machines that can produce different ice shapes and sizes. That's likely not the reality for home bartenders. For the purposes of this book, you will only need three ice shapes to make just about anything you want at home. The best ice has little to no impurities. If you feel like really nerding out and making crystal clear ice, boil your water, let it cool, and then freeze it; or use distilled water.

- 1¼-inch (3 cm) cubes—These are the workhorses. They can be used for building, shaking, and stirring and are easily crushed for drinks that call for it. Many companies make easy-to-use silicone trays in this size. We like the ones from Peak the most, but just about anything off Amazon will do.

- 2-inch (5 cm) cubes—You'll need a larger rock for drinks that you want to slowly evolve over time. We like a standard 2-inch (5 cm) cube, but if you prefer a sphere, you do you.

- Crushed ice—If you're making a bunch of juleps or mojitos, it's well worth it to buy some crushed ice at the convenience store or local spot. Otherwise, take your small cubes, put them in a dish towel, and pound them with a mallet or rolling pin.

TOOLS

—●—

Speed Rack is pretty lo-fi when it comes to tools. The space constraints of the stage mean we have to keep ingredient lists and gear fairly limited, though we've been amazed by the creativity we've seen over the years, especially with garniture—decked out citrus twists and a palm tree garnish made from a cinnamon stick and a sprig of mint still stand out. For the purposes of this book, it'd be good to have a jigger or two and a couple of strainers, and, if you're feeling fancy, a muddler (though a wooden spoon handle will absolutely do the trick).

JIGGERS

There are two methods for measuring cocktail ingredients, one art, the other science. The first, "free pouring," involves bartenders counting out their pours, rather than using a tool to measure. And the other (which tends to be more precise, though we have seen some insanely fine-tuned free pourers) utilizes what we call jiggers, in essence a small double-sided measuring cup. We recommend getting one that has a 1-ounce (30 ml) and a 2-ounce (60 ml) side and another with a ½-ounce (15 ml) and ¾-ounce (22.5 ml) side for top efficiency.

STRAINERS

Using a strainer when pouring drinks from a shaker or mixing glass serves a few purposes: First, it holds the ice back. Second, it will keep any ice chips out of the drink. And third, in the case of fine strainers, it will keep sediment, fruit pulp and seeds, herbs, etc. out of the final product for a much smoother drink. You'll want two types of strainers: a Hawthorne (that's the one with the coil) and a fine strainer (of the conical mesh variety). Some recipes in the book call for double straining, in which case you'll use both of your strainers at once for next-level clarity.

GLASSWARE

—●—

If you love collecting glasses (and we do), go for it! Get a bunch of shapes and sizes. Below are what you'll need for the drinks in this book—anything else is extra credit.

COCKTAIL GLASS

For drinks served "up" you'll want a moderate-size glass with a stem. A coupe, martini glass, and a Nick & Nora are the classic shapes, but there's plenty of leeway to get playful.

ROCKS GLASS

Most drinks served "down" on the rocks will require a glass that's not much taller than it is wide, holding about 8 to 10 ounces (240 to 300 ml). Rocks or double old-fashioned glasses will do the trick.

TALL GLASS

These are for long drinks, usually called a highball or a Collins. You'll want something that can hold 10 to 12 ounces (300 to 360 ml), ice and cocktail all told.

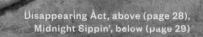

Disappearing Act, above (page 28),
Midnight Sippin', below (page 29)

CHAPTER 1

ALL DAY EVERY DAY

NO- AND LOW-ABV DRINKS

In more recent Speed Rack seasons, we have noticed that more and more judges are calling for less boozy takes on drinks. From brand-new creations to variations on spritzes and stirred sherry classics, the trend is clear: Sometimes we just want a little less alcohol in our glass. It's a movement that's gaining traction across bartending, to meet not only the demands of a more health-focused world, but also those of more mindful drinking. We're mixing lower alcohol and even completely non-alcoholic drinks into our drinking customs to keep intoxication at bay. Over the course of an evening, it's cool to have a low-ABV option like a Bamboo (page 258) to start, followed by a zero-proof "No-groni" (page 223), with a tropical old-fashioned (see Sian Buchan's La Isla Bonita, page 119) as a full strength nightcap. It's a way to keep our wits about us and make sure we feel good when we wake up in the morning. Cheers to that!

We have traveled to twenty-three cities in the US mainland and ten countries with Speed Rack, sampling cocktails from some of the best bars in the world at every stop. Considering how many drinks we consume, we're enthusiastically in support of the growing number of no- and low-alcohol cocktails that have been gaining prominence on menus everywhere. It's gone beyond a trend, becoming a category that's hard to keep up with, evolving even as we write this book. This momentum is central to our mission of inclusivity: More guests are being empowered to go into bars knowing that there will be something for them to sip. Today, anyone can participate in the drinks culture without feeling like they have to make excuses for their choices. We're happy to see the word "mocktail" vanishing from cocktail lists and non-alcoholic cocktails mixed in among the boozy ones. As far as we're concerned—a drink is a drink is a drink.

Over the last decade, creating cocktails that are low in alcohol has moved way past the Aperol spritz; there's a real art to dialing back the booze and still finding balance and refreshment. Some of the thought leaders in this category are Speed Rack alums. Competitors like Natasha David and Julia Momosé have become poster women for low-proof cocktails—using ingredients like vermouth, sherry, sparkling wine, sake, and shochu to great effect.

The Low-Alc Toolkit

————•————

This movement coincides with a wider access to these ingredients. Take fortified wines, like sherry. Back at the turn of the twentieth century, these were wildly popular, consumed by all because they were way, way better than higher-proof spirits. Distillation wasn't always all that great at the time and sticking to wines that were perfected in their fortification for transatlantic transportation was frequently the smarter and tastier choice. It was around that time that the Bamboo and the Sherry Cobbler were created—

sherry was in vogue (as were its cousins port and Madeira). And then it wasn't. And now it is again. (Bartenders rejoice!) From salty, citrusy finos to oxidized ones like amontillados and dark, toasty olorosos, sherries make fantastic bases for lower-proof creations, such as Tess Anne Sawyer's brilliant Prima Donna (page 48), which combines nutty amontillado-style sherry with sweet, fruity East India sherry from Lustau.

And then there's vermouth. With wine as their base, vermouth can bring citrus, herbs, and other botanicals in many different flavorful combinations. Not only are imports from France, Italy, and Spain on the rise, but there are also vermouth booms in the US, Australia, Argentina, and beyond underway. Similarly, the category of amaro (from Italy, yes, but the world over, too) has grown immensely, and while these digestifs do often have a bit higher ABV, they are also flavor-packed and bring their own sugar, which means they can make a statement, even in small amounts. Used in lower-proof cocktails, a modifier (bar speak for an alcohol-based ingredient that brings more flavor to a cocktail's base spirit) like amaro can be the star of its own show rather than a supporting character.

Fermented ingredients like kombucha and tepache (made from pineapple rind and piloncillo) make smart substitutes for beer or sparkling wine in drinks that are in search of a fermented vibe. Just note that these often have a little alcohol, some up to 3%, so they will not work in non-alcoholic constructions.

The Art of the Split Base

————•————

With a deeper back bar in these categories, bartenders have more ways to tame the alcohol in drinks. One way is to split the base of a cocktail with a high-proof spirit and one of these lower-proof fortified wines, sakes, or shochu. This lowers the drink's ABV by using only 1 ounce (30 ml) of a 40%+ spirit instead of the usual 2 ounces (60 ml), as in a 50/50 martini. Another way is inverting proportions in classic drinks, as in a Reverse Manhattan, made with 2 ounces (60 ml) of sweet vermouth and 1 ounce (30 ml) of whiskey with a few dashes of bitters.

One benefit of knowing the classics inside and out is that you can tinker with dependable templates as desired to reduce the alcohol. Take an old-school sour template (2 parts spirit : ¾ citrus : ¾ sugar), like a gimlet or a daiquiri: it's easy enough to swap out full-proof spirits for those that aren't. We love a sherry daiquiri that leaves out the high-proof spirit rum all together, made with 2 ounces (60 ml) fino sherry, ¾ ounce (22.5 ml) simple syrup, and ¾ ounce (22.5 ml) lime. The fino has the same lightness as white rum, but with a mouthwatering salinity that gives the drink a serious crushability.

Zeroing in on Zero Proof

As for those who want to drink cocktails without consuming alcohol at all, the options are far greater than they've ever been. There are amazing resources, like retail shop Boisson, that have curated the best non-alcoholic products across the US and online. Gone are the days of sticky-sweet, glorified lemonades dressed up with mint sprigs. We'd argue that zero-proof drinks require bartenders to dig further into the realm of experimentation to achieve the complex textures, bite, aromas, and acid expected in drinks at the best cocktail bars.

From this new canon of alcohol-free drinks has emerged an entirely new category of non-alcoholic "spirits" that are distilled to concentrate flavor, but not alcohol. Over the last few years, a plethora of companies have launched zero-proof gins, tequilas, whiskeys, and more, bringing an unexplored frontier of flavor. And just because these products are booze-free, it doesn't mean that their use is exclusive to non-alcoholic drinks. They can be used to lower the alcohol content in any drink or to bring in flavors that ordinarily can't be achieved without booze.

Just know that mixing with these ingredients is different from mixing with the punch of alcohol; you'll need rethink old routines. For example, because non-alcoholic "spirits" lack the heat and viscosity of alcohol, they don't require dilution, which means you will probably need to limit any shaking or stirring in order to help retain their flavor intensity within a drink. To this end, consider storing these ingredients in the fridge to keep them cold without watering them down.

Flavor Infusions

A low-lift way to add more layers to no- and low-alcohol drinks is with flavored simple syrups and infusions. We have numerous iterations in this book that can be used in myriad ways. For example, Lydia McLuen's Fennel Syrup (page 69) is a perfect stand-in for absinthe; Leanne Favre's Hibiscus Bitter (page 224) can be used in place of Campari. For something moodier, a syrup made from smoky lapsang souchong tea (page 261) will bring mezcal- and scotch-like wisps of smoke. And then Mony Bunni's Arabic Tea Syrup (page 90) is a no-brainer swap for allspice dram and will be a friend to any drink that's normally made with barrel-aged spirits like whiskey and rum.

We don't have it all figured out just yet, but we're excited by all of the experimentation and development in this area. Have an open mind and show us what you've got.

We want something
festive, but also light
and savory. Disco,
bubbles, and fun in a
glass, please!

CREATOR

NATASHA DAVID
Speed Rack competitor

ABV: 13%

1 ounce (30 ml) Lillet Blanc

½ ounce (15 ml) aquavit,
preferably Linie

½ ounce (15 ml) lemon juice

½ ounce (15 ml) Simple
Syrup (page 262)

1 teaspoon Giffard Pêche de
Vigne liqueur

2 ounces (60 ml) sparkling
wine

Lemon twist, for garnish

DISAPPEARING ACT

"Being part of the inaugural Speed Rack crew was life changing," Natasha told us. "I was able to forge lasting friendships, develop professional relationships, and gain confidence," she said. Something tells us her star was already rising: In the ten years since she first competed in Speed Rack, she's owned disco ball- and owl-adorned New York City bar Nitecap, consulted on countless cocktail programs, and authored a book called *Drink Lightly*, which is filled with the sorts of low-ABV cocktails that she's become so well-known for. The Disappearing Act (photo on page 24) takes notes from a classic French 75 (page 255), with Lillet Blanc as the base to dial back the booze. "I adore working with fortified wines," she said. "They present a whole different set of challenges compared to more traditional base spirits." She combines this with the earthy, savory notes of aquavit and the bouncy juiciness of peach liqueur, topping it off with ice-cold, dry bubbles.

HOW TO MAKE THE DRINK

Add all the ingredients, except the sparkling wine, to a cocktail shaker filled with ice. Shake until cold and fine strain into a chilled coupe. Top with the sparkling wine. Express the lemon twist over the drink, place it in the glass, and serve.

MIDNIGHT SIPPIN'

CREATOR

LAUREN "LP" PAYLOR O'BRIEN
Speed Rack competitor

ABV: 0%

1½ ounces (45 ml) Seedlip Grove 42 distilled non-alcoholic spirit

1½ ounces (45 ml) white verjus

½ ounce (15 ml) Five-Spiced Honey Syrup (recipe follows)

3 ounces (90 ml) soda water, to top

Lemon twist and a rosemary sprig, for garnish

When Lauren Paylor O'Brien won the first season of Netflix's *Drink Masters*, the whole world came to know something that we've known at Speed Rack for years: LP's a superstar. She competed in Speed Rack in Washington, D.C., in Season 8, and is a member of our Speed Rack Advisory Squad. And in 2020 she and Speed Rack alum Alex Jump (see page 182) joined forces and founded Focus on Health (FOH to those in the know), an organization that aims to help people in the hospitality industry take care of *themselves* both physically and mentally. Of late, she's been exploring non-alcoholic drinks more. "Drinking for an occasion can be a difficult thing to do in a mindful manner," she tells us. With this completely booze-free cocktail (photo on page 24), her goal was to mimic the texture, flavor, and carbonation of sparkling wine, so that everyone, even those avoiding alcohol, can feel part of the celebration. Here, LP brilliantly uses a spice-infused honey syrup and verjus (a brightly acidic pressed juice made from not-quite-ripe wine grapes) to add layers of flavor similar to what you'd find in sparkling wine. Many new non-alc products have emerged on the scene to offer alternatives to alcohol, but Seedlip led the charge. In this cocktail, LP calls on Seedlip's aperitivo-esque Grove bottling for its citrus notes and soda water to provide the bubbles. Because there's no ice involved in the making of this drink, be sure all of your ingredients are cold before mixing.

HOW TO MAKE THE DRINK

Add all the ingredients to a chilled champagne flute and stir gently with a spoon to combine. Express the lemon twist over the drink and discard. Garnish with the rosemary sprig and serve.

Five-Spiced Honey Syrup

Makes about 1½ cups (360 ml)

2 to 3 star anise pods (6 g)

1 tablespoon (6 g) whole cloves

1 teaspoon (2 g) fennel seeds

2 cinnamon sticks, crushed

1½ teaspoons (3 g) Szechuan peppercorns

1 cup (240 ml) Simple Syrup (page 262)

½ cup (120 ml) honey, preferably elderflower

Toast the spices in a saucepan over low heat until fragrant. Add the simple syrup and honey and simmer over low heat for 5 minutes while stirring. Remove from the heat and pour into an airtight container. Let the syrup infuse at room temperature for 24 hours and then fine strain. Store in the refrigerator for up to 1 month.

DEALER'S
CHOICE

Give us a no-ABV,
herbaceous
springtime sour on
the rocks.

THE SECRET GARDEN

Whether she was serving St-Germain punch to a thirsty audience, onstage hustling in Season 7, or mentoring rising star competitors, Una Green has been an undeniably important staple of Speed Rack—and of the Los Angeles cocktail scene. She is also, unfortunately, one of our competitors who has been directly affected by breast cancer. But it has never stopped her from showing up with her encouraging spirit. Una worked at our San Francisco competition in 2019 while in the middle of treatment, and she attended our 2020 Denver event just shortly after finishing. Her cocktail shared here is a lush, green, well-balanced sour, exactly as requested. "It gives me garden margarita vibes," Una says. It's based on an herb-inflected non-alcoholic spirit from Seedlip, a pioneer in the category. To complement it, Una recommends only using a pinch of dill, as it can be overpowering. "We want the flavors of each ingredient to balance each other harmoniously," she says.

CREATOR

UNA GREEN
Speed Rack competitor

ABV: 0%

---

6 fresh mint leaves

1 pinch fresh dill fronds

2 slices cucumber

2 ounces (60 ml) Seedlip Garden 108 distilled non-alcoholic spirit

¾ ounce (22.5 ml) lemon juice

¾ ounce (22.5 ml) Smoked Salt Simple Syrup (recipe follows)

Mint and dill bouquet, cucumber wheel, black pepper, and flaky sea salt, for garnish

HOW TO MAKE THE DRINK

Add the mint, dill, and cucumber to a cocktail shaker and muddle. Add the Seedlip, lemon juice, and simple syrup. Shake until cold and strain into a rocks glass filled with ice. Garnish with the herb bouquet, cucumber wheel, a sprinkle of black pepper, and salt. Serve.

Smoked Salt Simple Syrup

Makes about 1½ cups (360 ml)

---

1 cup (200 g) granulated sugar

1 teaspoon smoked salt, preferably Maldon

1 bay leaf

Combine all the ingredients with 1 cup (240 ml) water in a saucepan. Over low heat, stir until the sugar and salt are dissolved. Remove from the heat. Once cooled, discard the bay leaf and pour the syrup into an airtight container. Store in the refrigerator for up to 2 weeks. This syrup is delicious dashed into margaritas, should you have any left over.

DEALER'S CHOICE

———

We'd like a white wine spritzer, but better than what our moms used to drink. Make us a creative version of this classic crusher.

UNFATON

MELINA MEZA
Speed Rack competitor

———

ABV: 19%

———

2 ounces (60 ml) Tahitian Vanilla Bean–Infused Martini & Rossi Fiero aperitivo (recipe follows)

1½ ounces (45 ml) cantaloupe juice (see Note)

1 ounce (30 ml) Fever-Tree Sparkling Pink Grapefruit Soda

3 ounces (90 ml) light-bodied white wine, preferably txakolina

Orange Blossom Water Solution (recipe follows)

Cantaloupe or assorted melon cubes, a grapefruit half wheel, and a bouquet of mint sprigs, for garnish

WEISER SPRITZ

Consider this spritzer a tribute to ultra-ripe, peak-summer fruit. Melina has a knack for spritzes and they're some of her favorite drinks to make. For this one, she uses the traditional Aperol spritz specs (3 parts sparkling wine:2 parts Aperol:1 part soda water) but adds freshly juiced cantaloupe. She uses melons from Weiser Farms in California's Central Valley, saying, "They're the sweetest, most juicy and delicious melons you will ever have." That said, you can use any cantaloupe, but the riper the better! This is combined with a vanilla bean–infused red bitter aperitivo called Martini & Rossi Fiero to make a cocktail that she says reminds her of an Orange Julius. (Stir any leftover infused Fiero into a vanilla-scented Negroni [page 223] or shake into a Jungle Bird [page 256] for added depth.) A dose of lightly fizzy Basque white wine, a quick spray of orange blossom water, and a couple melon cubes gild the lily. Build this spritz in a wine glass, adding ice at the very end so that the flavors can all come together in something she calls "complex and crushable." We agree.

HOW TO MAKE THE DRINK

Add the infused Martini & Rossi Fiero, cantaloupe juice, grapefruit soda, and wine to a large wine glass. Fill the glass with ice. Using an atomizer (see Tools in Resources, page 259), spritz the top of the drink with the orange blossom water. Garnish with a couple of cantaloupe and melon cubes, a grapefruit half wheel, and a bouquet of mint and serve with a straw.

NOTE To make the cantaloupe juice, cut the rind off a small melon, remove the seeds, and slice it into cubes. Place in a blender and blend until smooth. Pour the juice through a fine-mesh strainer to remove any pulp.

Tahitian Vanilla Bean–Infused Martini & Rossi Fiero

Makes 16 ounces (480 ml)

1 Tahitian vanilla bean

2 cups (480 ml) Martini & Rossi Fiero aperitivo

Pour the Martini & Rossi Fiero into an airtight container. Slice the vanilla bean in half lengthwise and place it inside the bottle of Martini & Rossi Fiero. Shake well. Let steep for at least 24 hours, shaking every so often, until your desired vanilla flavor is achieved. Strain through a fine-mesh sieve and discard the vanilla bean. Store in the refrigerator for up to 1 month.

Orange Blossom Water Solution

Makes about 2 ounces (60 ml)

1 teaspoon orange blossom water

Combine the orange blossom water with 2 ounces (60 ml) water in an atomizer. Shake. Will keep for up to 6 months at room temperature.

CREATOR

MISTY KALKOFEN
Speed Rack judge

ABV: 23%

---

1 ounce (30 ml) mezcal,
preferably Del Maguey Vida

1 ounce (30 ml) St-Germain
elderflower liqueur

½ ounce (15 ml) Punt e Mes

½ ounce (15 ml) lemon juice

Lemon twist, for garnish

MAXIMILIAN AFFAIR

Shout out to the great Misty Kalkofen! One of the OGs in our bar world, Misty, the "Madrina of Mezcal," was the president and founder of the Boston chapter of LUPEC (Ladies United for the Preservation of Endangered Cocktails) back in the mid-aughts and was one of our north stars in founding Speed Rack. A bar feminist through and through, she's been researching the impact that women have had on drinking culture throughout history and co-authored *Drinking Like Ladies*, which if you like *this* book, we highly recommend you pick up, too. Today, some bartenders might look at the specs for this drink and question whether it's actually low-alc, but when she conceived the Maximilian Affair in 2008, with only an ounce of smoky mezcal, rounded out with floral St-Germain and bitter Punt e Mes vermouth, it was, indeed, an ahead-of-its time low-alcohol drink. This modern classic is now found on cocktail menus across the globe.

HOW TO MAKE THE DRINK

Add all the ingredients to a cocktail shaker filled with ice. Shake until cold and strain into a chilled cocktail glass. Express the lemon twist over the drink, place it in the glass, and serve.

FROM THE
FOUNDERS
———

Make this for dirty
vodka martini
drinkers or anyone
who wants a savory
cocktail sans alcohol.

CREATOR

LYNNETTE
MARRERO
Speed Rack co-founder

ABV: 0%

2 ounces (60 ml) Olive Oil–
Washed Seedlip Garden–
Amass Riverine Blend
(page 261)

½ ounce (15 ml) Roots
Divino non-alcoholic
Aperitif Bianco (see
Non-Alcoholic Spirits in
Resources, page 259)

½ ounce (15 ml) Seasoned
Olive Brine (page 262)

Lemon twist and an herb-
brined olive skewered on a
rosemary sprig, for garnish

PLAN AHEAD

BETTY DRAPER MARTINI

This was inspired by an impressive zero-proof dirty martini I watched bartender Carina Soto Velasquez, of Paris cocktail bar Candelaria fame, whip up at a competition in London in 2015. I wanted to make my own version. Suffice to say that it would have been nearly impossible to make this drink a decade ago, before the boom in non-alcoholic distilled spirits. But today, we are lucky to have access to some remarkable ingredients that make something like a booze-free martini relatively easy. For this, I've combined the non-alcoholic distilled spirits Seedlip Garden and Amass Riverine, both of which are made using botanicals that are signatures of gin, as well as a no-alc aperitif that comes very close to dry vermouth. Fat washing (that is infusing fat, be it oil, butter, lard, bacon grease into a spirit) is a method that's become popular among bartenders looking to add more weight and texture to their drinks, and it's a tool that I've found useful for achieving the right mouthfeel in non-alcoholic drinks. For this martini, I fat wash the Seedlip with grassy olive oil to bring the necessary slinkiness to the cocktail. I've also made a seasoned olive brine to add an herbal dimension to this beautifully cloudy drink. It's named for the true star of the show *Mad Men*, January Jones, aka Betty Draper, who spent a season drinking plenty of martinis while pregnant.

HOW TO MAKE THE DRINK

Add all the ingredients to a mixing glass filled with ice. Stir until cold and strain into a small martini glass or coupe. Express the lemon twist over the drink and discard. Garnish with the skewered olive and serve.

DEALER'S CHOICE

———

We want an Italian vacation in Mexico. Take us to Roma!

CREATOR

PRISCILLA LEONG
Speed Rack competitor, Australia winner

ABV: 11%

¾ ounce (22.5 ml) blanco tequila

¾ ounce (22.5 ml) dry vermouth

½ ounce (15 ml) Campari

¾ ounce (22.5 ml) lime juice

½ ounce (15 ml) Simple Syrup (page 262)

2 ounces (60 ml) soda water

Lime wedge and a sprig of basil or mint, for garnish

NORTH BEACH COOLER

"I've always loved a speed challenge and there haven't been many bartending events in Australia that have given us girls a reason to get together for a great cause," says Priscilla Leong. With this competitive edge and a close family member who has battled breast cancer, "How could I say no?" she asks. She was the very first winner of Speed Rack Australia. Priscilla is in the business of making lower-alcohol drinks that, in her words, "still deliver a huge flavor punch." Because she herself has an alcohol allergy, she's always looking to drinks that are less boozy and that will pair well with food. For this tall cooler, she followed the roadmap for modern classic Rome with a View (page 258): Campari, dry vermouth, lime, simple syrup, and soda water. Here she splits the base with tequila and Campari and garnishes with basil, for something that can go from day into night. When it comes to getting the balance of tartness and sweetness right, Priscilla emphasizes the importance of tasting your cocktails as you make them, especially when fresh fruit juice is involved: "All fruits vary in sweetness depending on the season."

HOW TO MAKE THE DRINK

Add all the ingredients, except the soda water, to a shaker filled with ice. Shake until cold and strain into a chilled highball glass. Top with the soda water, fill the glass with ice, and garnish with a wedge of lime and a sprig of basil or mint. Serve.

DEALER'S CHOICE

———

Micheladas are some of our favorite low-alcohol cocktails. Can you make us a special sangrita to mix with beer for your own unique riff?

CARROT PAPAYA MICHELADA

An early-years competitor, Shannon Ponche admits she's met most of her bosses—Ivy, Julie Reiner, Natasha David, and Leo Robitschek—through Speed Rack. They've been so lucky to have her. She is arguably one of the masters of savory cocktails, not to mention the fact that she is a joy to watch working behind a bar. This drink asked her to reimagine the average michelada, a classic Mexican beer cocktail combining a light lager, lime juice, and sangrita, a savory drink made with tomato and chiles that's often served alongside sipping tequila. This drink is fruity and perfectly spicy and has found a very devoted following at Leyenda in Brooklyn where, it is the house michelada recipe. Shannon's sangrita forgoes tomato altogether; it's a concoction of sweet papaya puree (see the fruit puree sources in the Resources, page 259) with earthy carrot and tangy lime and orange juices, kicked up with guajillo and chipotle chiles.

CREATOR

SHANNON PONCHE
Speed Rack competitor, regional winner

———

ABV: 3%

———

Fine sea salt, for rim

2 ounces (60 ml) Carrot Papaya Sangrita (recipe follows)

8 ounces (240 ml) Mexican lager, such as Pacifico or Negra Modelo

Fine sea salt and a lime wedge, for garnish

HOW TO MAKE THE DRINK

Rim a pint glass with salt and fill with ice. Pour the sangrita into the glass and top with the beer. Stir, garnish with the lime wedge, and serve.

Carrot Papaya Sangrita
Makes 14 ounces (420 ml)

---

6 ounces (180 ml) papaya puree (see Resources, page 259)

6 ounces (180 ml) carrot juice

1 ounce (30 ml) lime juice

1 ounce (30 ml) orange juice

½ teaspoon ground guajillo chile (see Resources, page 259)

¼ teaspoon ground chipotle chile (see Resources, page 259)

¼ teaspoon fine sea salt

Combine all the ingredients in an airtight container and stir to incorporate. Store in the refrigerator for up to 1 week.

FROM THE FOUNDERS
—

Make this for your friend who wants a little bitterness without the booze at the tail end of Dry January.

CREATOR

IVY MIX
Speed Rack co-founder

ABV: 0%

½ lemon, quartered

½ ounce (15 ml) Simple Syrup (page 262)

5 to 7 fresh mint leaves

2 ounces (60 ml) The Pathfinder Hemp and Root (see Non-Alcoholic Spirits in Resources, page 259)

Lemon wheel and mint sprig, for garnish

FEATHERWEIGHT SMASH

For most bartenders, when they hear the words "bitter and slammable," what probably comes to mind is some sort of spritz riff—and with good reason, as there are so many non-alcoholic aperitifs available now. I, however, decided to lean into the smash template—a cousin of the sour that's made with muddled citrus rather than juiced. This cocktail is an homage to the Prizefighter Smash created by Nick Jarrett, which was on the menu for years while we worked together at Brooklyn's Clover Club. The original drink was low ABV before low ABV was cool, based on Fernet and Carpano Antica. For this version, I used The Pathfinder Hemp and Root, a booze-free take on amaro, made with many herbs, spices, and roots that show up in traditional amari, as well as hemp. It's a favorite of mine for no-, low-, and even full-ABV drinks with a richness that's matched by bitterness, thanks to the tannins from the hemp plant. (And no, it won't get you high, it's THC- and CBD-free, too.) A tip: When muddling the lemon here, you're just looking to bruise it to release the bright oils in the skin, not destroy it. For that same reason, the more delicate mint is added just before shaking. And if your lemon is super hard, it won't be very juicy; if that's the case, squeeze in a little extra fresh juice to make up for it.

HOW TO MAKE THE DRINK

Add the lemon and simple syrup to a cocktail shaker and muddle gently. Add the mint leaves and The Pathfinder and fill the shaker with ice. Shake until cold and fine strain into a double rocks glass over crushed ice. Garnish with the lemon wheel and mint sprig, and serve.

Make this for
wine lovers and
spiced-rum fans.

CREATOR

**LYNNETTE
MARRERO**
Speed Rack co-founder

ABV: 0%

2 ounces (60 ml) red verjus
(see Resources, page 259)

1½ ounces (45 ml) Seedlip
Spice 94 distilled non-
alcoholic spirit

¾ ounce (22.5 ml)
pineapple juice

½ ounce (15 ml) Cinnamon
Syrup (page 260)

Pineapple leaf, for garnish

Red grapes, for garnish

TALK TO HER

Named after a Pedro Almodóvar film featuring the Spanish actor Penelope Cruz, this sangria riff is one I made for a bar that didn't yet have its liquor license, but had plans to focus on wine-based drinks once they did. As such, I temporarily subbed in red verjus (a brightly acidic pressed juice made from not-quite-ripe wine grapes) for red wine, but wound up almost liking it more this way. I wanted to infuse this sangria with lots of warming spices, and for that I tapped non-alcoholic Seedlip Spice 94, which is made with allspice and green cardamom. It's an ingredient that I've also been known to use in drinks that *do* contain alcohol because it's a very easy way to get lots of flavor without having to make my own infusions. For a little boost in texture and body, I use ½ ounce (15 ml) of cinnamon syrup. This drink can be made in single-serve portions or in a pitcher for a party (see Note). And should you want to punch it up, it's fantastic with ¾ ounce (22.5 ml) rum or pisco—or even ½ ounce (15 ml) of each.

HOW TO MAKE THE DRINK

Add all the ingredients to a rocks glass filled with ice. Give it a quick stir, garnish with some red grapes and a pineapple leaf in each, and serve.

NOTE   To make a large batch of this sangria (about six 5-ounce [150 ml] servings), combine 16 ounces (480 ml) red verjus, 10 ounces (300 ml) Seedlip Spice 94, 5 ounces (150 ml) pineapple juice, and 4 ounces (120 ml) cinnamon syrup in a pitcher. Stir until incorporated and serve in rocks glasses over ice, with a pineapple leaf and a skewer with red grapes in each.

DEALER'S
CHOICE

———

Could we have a
low-proof, stirred,
savory drink,
served up?

CREATOR

JULIA MOMOSÉ
Speed Rack competitor

———

ABV: 20%

¼ ounce (7.5 ml) Beniimosu
Syrup (recipe follows)

¼ ounce (7.5 ml) Armagnac,
preferably Marie Duffau
Napoleon

½ ounce (15 ml) umeshu,
preferably Nanbu Bijin

½ ounce (15 ml) shochu,
preferably Nishi Shuzo
Tenshi no Yuwaku Imo

1½ ounces (45 ml) junmai
sake, preferably Kokuryu
Kuzuryu

Orange twist, for garnish

TRIPTYCH

Because Speed Rack is all about lightning-fast drinks execution, garnishes, beyond the compulsory citrus twist or herbs here or there, never really played much of a role in the competition—until Julia Momosé came along. Her drinks always have thoughtful aesthetics, on top of being delicious. Born and raised in Japan, Julia is the owner of Chicago's bar Kumiko and author of *The Way of the Cocktail* (which won a James Beard Award in 2022), both of which highlight Japanese ingredients and bartending techniques, with an emphasis on lower-alcohol cocktails. Here, Julia combines several Japanese ingredients, umeshu (plum liqueur), shochu (a distilled clear spirit, most often from rice or barley, sweet potatoes, and beyond), sake, and a vibrant syrup, made from Japanese purple sweet potato vinegar with just ¼ ounce (7.5 ml) Armagnac. Most of these ingredients are widely available now, but the vinegar is a bit trickier—it can be purchased from the Japanese Pantry (thejapanesepantry.com). And while we were a bit surprised that there's no garnish for this drink, considering her legacy, we'll count its rose gold hue as such.

HOW TO MAKE THE DRINK

Add all the ingredients to a mixing glass filled with ice. Stir until cold and strain into a chilled cocktail glass. Express the orange twist over the drink, discard, and serve.

Beniimosu Syrup

Makes approximately 1½ cups (360 ml)

¼ cup (60 ml) Beniimosu
purple sweet potato
vinegar

1 cup (200 g) granulated
sugar

Combine the vinegar with ¾ cup (180 ml) water in an airtight container. Add the sugar and stir until completely dissolved. Cover and store in the refrigerator for up to 3 weeks.

DEALER'S CHOICE

We would love a low-ABV nightcap. Send us off to sweet dreams without nightmares for tomorrow.

CREATOR

TESS ANNE SAWYER

Speed Rack competitor, USA national winner

ABV: 19%

¾ ounce (22.5 ml) amontillado sherry

¾ ounce (22.5 ml) Lustau East India sherry

¾ ounce (22.5 ml) dry vermouth

¾ ounce (22.5 ml) sweet vermouth

2 dashes Angostura bitters

2 dashes orange bitters

Lemon twist, for garnish

PRIMA DONNA

Tess Anne Sawyer has participated in more Speed Rack competitions than nearly anyone. From the first time she stepped onstage, she wowed everyone with the precision and athleticism of her free-pouring technique. What is this you say? Well, a lot of cocktail bartenders choose to use jiggers as measuring tools to ensure accuracy. Tess, however, came from the high-volume New York City bar Mother's Ruin, where she honed her free-pouring skills to perfection. From the moment she took the stage, Speed Rack began to shift and today we see a combination of free pouring *and* jiggering to ensure speed and accuracy. This drink was one she devised for her final round in New York City in 2015. Judge Julie Reiner asked for a sherry-based cocktail and Tess knew exactly what to make—a drink that she'd been serving at Mother's Ruin to industry friends when they came by post shift. "During that time, I had recently discovered the Adonis and Bamboo cocktails and I was in love," she explained. This drink is an outrageous mash-up of the two. In addition to dry, nutty amontillado sherry, Tess adds an equal measure of Lustau's East India sherry, which has sweet dried-fruit flavors. It's a study in incredible balance and a true celebration of the potential of sherry.

HOW TO MAKE THE DRINK

Add all the ingredients to a mixing glass filled with ice. Stir until cold and strain into a chilled Nick & Nora glass. Express the lemon twist over the drink and place it in the glass; serve.

FALL FREE

I'm obsessed with the fall—the colorful leaves, the chill in the air, the apples, and an excuse to have a warm drink every night, if I so choose. Here, I wanted to make an autumnal sipper that could be served both hot and cold. What I love about it is that you can batch it and keep it in the fridge and then serve it up however you like, whenever you like. Whereas I generally steer clear of flavored vodkas in my cocktail making, the zero proof CleanCo Apple vodka really makes the drink sing. It's like an amped up mulled cider without the work of mulling! I created this recipe to fit the non-alcoholic bill, but you can certainly add a little rum or bourbon for a boozy kick, if you so desire.

CREATOR

IVY MIX
Speed Rack co-founder

ABV: 0%

---

2 ounces (60 ml) CleanCo Apple Vodka Alternative (see Resources, page 259)

2½ ounces (75 ml) apple cider

½ ounce (15 ml) lemon juice

½ ounce (15 ml) maple syrup

Apple fan and cinnamon stick, for garnish

HOW TO MAKE THE DRINK

For the cold version: Add all the ingredients to a cocktail shaker filled with ice. Shake and strain into a highball glass over fresh ice. Garnish with the apple fan and cinnamon stick and serve.

For the hot version: Add all the ingredients to a small pot over low heat. Warm until steaming and hot but not boiling. Pour into a warmed mug. Garnish with the apple fan and cinnamon stick and serve.

Emcee for Speed Rack Midwest, Season 6, Robin Nance

BACK THE RACK
Our Commitment to Fighting Breast Cancer

Standing on stage in front of 650 people in Chicago's Thalia Hall, with the whole room chanting "Fuck Cancer!" is a vibe. It's certainly unlike any other breast cancer charity event we've ever attended and it's 1,000 percent Speed Rack. And if the name of our competition and our logo weren't big enough clues, Speed Rack is a feminist, pro-boob organization.

Since we launched Speed Rack in 2011, we've raised more than $1.75 million for breast cancer charities globally. It is entirely thanks to our incredibly generous and devoted sponsors that we can donate every dollar—from the ticket costs, to the t-shirts, to the tips dropped in bowls on the sponsor's bars—directly to breast cancer research, education, and awareness. Throughout the years we have contributed to SHARE, The Pink Agenda, The National Breast Cancer Foundation, Dana Farber, and others in the United States, as well as International organizations like Taller Salud in Puerto Rico and Fundación de Cáncer de Mama in Mexico.

Breast cancer affects more women than almost any disease. In a competition that's centered around women bartenders, there was no way breast cancer wasn't going to be a part of the conversation. We've always said that if it's not your mom, it's your best friend's mom who has it; it's less than 7 degrees of separation; it's one or two. Most people have a connection to breast cancer, and it doesn't take long to find it. A handful of competitors have had breast cancer over the years—and statistics tell us that more will in the coming years—and many, many more have family members or friends who they compete in honor of.

One of our most successful fundraising cities is Chicago. Events there are always jam-packed and vibrant—even during the cold Chicago winters. One of our favorite Windy City judges is Bridget Albert who was born and raised outside the city. She comes from a long line of women bartenders and has been a mentor to many in Chicago. Back in 2014, a close friend of Bridget's died of breast cancer, leaving behind several children. We decided to put some of the money raised that year to her hospice in her family's name and her family attended Speed Rack the next year. "It was a nice bright spot in a really dark time for my friend's family," Bridget says. We can't have an event in Chicago without Bridget, and she always brings the room to tears with the story of her friend. "When Speed Rack first came to Chicago," she says, "for me, personally, it was one of those most marvelous moments of my life to see women supporting women, and men supporting women and rooting them on, and doing something bigger than the cocktails that they were making." We feel just the same way.

Katie Renshaw with her Stolen Diamonds (page 57)

CELEBRATE
GOOD TIMES ...
COME ON!

DRINKS MADE BETTER WITH BUBBLY

Champagne and bubbles are synonymous with celebration, and to us, the best cocktails for getting a party started (and keeping it going) are those topped with sparkling wine. The drinks in this chapter are the liquid emojis of the cocktail world: glasses clinking, exploding Champagne bottles, and party horns shooting confetti.

These are *occasion* cocktails. New job? Big birthday? Or perhaps you're just happy to have made it all the way to Wednesday, whatever the case, break out the bubbly.

The operative word here is "royale." In the cocktail world, when you put Champagne on something, it's a "_____ royale," signifying that it's royalty, baby! Just about any cocktail can be royale-d, from a Kir to a Southside to a Sherry Cobbler (page 258). The classic French 75 is just a Tom Collins (gin, lemon, sugar) topped up with Champagne. And an Air Mail, basically a daiquiri with rum, honey, and a zap of lime, is essentially a royale d beach vacation in a glass.

The Golden Era of Sparkling Wine

Consider the classic Champagne cocktail: a sugar cube, a few dashes of aromatic bitters, and bubbles to top. But do you really need to pull out that luxe bottle of Dom Perignon you've been stashing away in your fridge for a French 75? You're more than welcome to, but these days it's easy to find something that fits the profile of dry (*brut* in French) and perfectly bubbly without breaking the bank.

We are truly in the golden era of sparkling wine. From South Africa to Italy to New Mexico and everywhere in between, winemakers all over the world are working in what's called *méthode Champenoise* or the Champagne method, with great results. And the options don't stop there! There is a sea of other sparklers, from frothy prosecco to deep red Lambrusco to cloudy pét-nats and even ciders and sparkling sake.

Each of these will have its own spectrum of bubbliness and sugar, so be sure to taste them first so that you can adjust your other specs accordingly.

With a sweeter prosecco, say, you might want to pull back on syrups or liqueurs to find balance in the drink. So, in the French 75 formula, rather than sticking to the usual 1½ ounces gin to ¾ ounces simple syrup and lemon, bring the simple down to ⅓ ounce to accommodate the sweetness of the wine. There are a couple of French 75 variations in this chapter (pages 61 and 71).

Alterna Bubbles

Outside of the wine realm, sparkling sake is an unexpected way to add a fruity, floral, and umami flourish to a cocktail. These often have the same ABV as sparkling wine and can range from dry to quite sweet, and have a little bit of fizz or be absolute bubble fountains. Which is to say: taste, taste, taste. We love to use them with tropical fruits, like passion fruit and pineapple, as well as drinks infused with tea to highlight some of the floral aromas. Lydia McLuen uses one with great success in her Place Setting (page 69), pairing it with both fennel and ginger syrups.

As for ciders—from the fruit-forward crisp styles from England and North America to the bolder, more wild styles of Normandy and the Basque region of Spain—they are a fresh way to bring even bigger fruit aromas to cocktails. Explore the full range! Not all ciders are made from apples; many producers will blend other fruits, including pears, quince, and cherries. Aside from fruitiness, some of the yeastier styles of cider can call forth a depth of umami and funkiness in a drink akin to something you might otherwise find in Jamaican rum.

Dress for the Occasion

If a party is in order, don't just pour your drinks into a Solo cup, go for a flute, a wine glass (stemmed or not, depending on the occasion), or a fancy, wide-bowled coupe on a skinny stem, the original Champagne vessel.

A note about measuring sparkling wine: we know that it's really annoying to do. It froths up, it loses bubbles, it's a mess. Eyeball it, we all do. And then get back to celebrating!

STOLEN DIAMONDS

CREATOR

KATIE RENSHAW
Speed Rack competitor, regional winner

---

1 ounce (30 ml) blanco tequila

1 ounce (30 ml) blanc vermouth

¼ ounce (7.5 ml) Campari

1 teaspoon apricot liqueur

1 teaspoon Hibiscus Grenadine (recipe follows)

2 ounces (60 ml) cava, to top

Grapefruit twist, for garnish

Katie was fairly new to competing (and bartending, actually) when she first took the stage at Speed Rack and wowed us with her skill and creativity. Drinks like this show why she's been so successful, not only in Speed Rack but in the global cocktail competition World Class, which she won representing the United States in 2019. This drink is thoughtfully layered in flavor, splitting the base between tequila and a perfumy lower-proof white vermouth, alongside citrusy Campari and apricot liqueur. Over the years, she's added in a fragrant, homemade hibiscus grenadine, which heightens the overall floral qualities. This has us dreaming of springtime and light, flowing dresses with glasses full of bubbles.

HOW TO MAKE THE DRINK

Add all the ingredients, except the cava, to a mixing glass filled with ice. Stir until cold. Strain into a chilled coupe and top with the cava. Express the grapefruit twist over the drink and place it in the glass; serve.

Hibiscus Grenadine

Makes about 1½ cups (360 ml)

---

1 cup (200 g) cane sugar

1 cup (240 ml) unsweetened pomegranate juice

¼ cup (10 g) dried hibiscus flowers (see Resources, page 259)

Add all the ingredients to a nonreactive saucepan. Warm over low heat until just below a simmer. Remove from the heat and steep for 15 to 20 minutes, whisking periodically to help dissolve the sugar. Strain and store in a glass bottle in the refrigerator for up to 3 weeks.

KNOW YOUR BUBBLES

CHAMPAGNE AND MÉTHODE CHAMPENOISE

The OG. From the northern France region of Champagne, these wines see a second fermentation in the bottle, which gives them their signature clean, consistent bubbles.

✧ **BEST IN:** If you're going to use *real* Champagne in a cocktail, use it in simpler drinks so that the Champagne is the highlight. Most Champagne is *brut* (dry), which makes it a killer blank canvas for juices, syrups, and any sweet modifiers. We love it with apricot, peach, and other stone fruit flavors.

PROSECCO

Made in northern Italy, just outside Venice, the home of the spritz, most prosecco sees its second fermentation in big, pressurized tanks, giving it bigger, frothy bubbles.

✧ **BEST IN:** Use prosecco in drinks that need big happy bubbles and a little winey flavor. With these we're leaning into Italian-style cocktails, like the spritz and Negroni Sbagliato.

CAVA

Spain's northeastern Penedes region adopted the Champagne style of winemaking 150 years ago. These wines are dependably dry and fresh with great acid. We'd argue cava is one of the most utilitarian of the sparklers and generally comes at an approachable price point.

✧ **BEST IN:** Any drink that needs an acid boost.

CRÉMANT

Crémants are from France, made in the Champagne method (and often with the same grape varieties), but outside the Champagne appellation. They're named for their region: Crémant de Bourgogne, Crémant de Alsace, etc. These wines are always much less pricey than Champagne, but have a similar dry, lively character.

✧ **BEST IN:** Any Champagne cocktail where you don't want to spring for Champagne.

LAMBRUSCO

Italy loves its bubbles. Lambrusco comes from Emilia-Romagna and is made in several different styles that can range from hot pink to crimson red in color and very sweet to bone dry on the palate. It's like a liqueur meets bubbles. Treat Lambrusco as a key ingredient not just a topper.

✧ **BEST IN:** Cocktails looking for some dark fruit or jammy flavors.

MOSCATO

Moscato, with its fragrant honeysuckle or orange blossom perfume, tends to be pretty sweet and has a softer bubble than other sparkling wines— it can often benefit from a little soda water too. Because the wine has so much of its own sweetness, you'll want to tone down any other added sugar in your cocktail.

✧ **BEST IN:** Fruity or floral drinks.

Beneath a champagne shower, Speed Rack Season 2 national champion Eryn Reece celebrates her win with emcee Chris Patino.

CREATOR

IVY MIX
Speed Rack co-founder

¾ ounce (22.5 ml) applejack, preferably Laird's Straight Apple Brandy—Bottled in Bond

¼ ounce (7.5 ml) Myris nutmeg liqueur

¼ ounce (7.5 ml) dark maple syrup

½ ounce (15 ml) lemon juice

1 dash Angostura bitters

2 ounces (60 ml) dry apple cider, such as Domaine Lesuffleur La Folletière, to top

Apple fan and lemon twist, for garnish

EYE APPLE

Should there be any question as to where I'm from, let this cocktail be the answer. As a Vermonter I have a lot of thoughts on autumnal libations and that the sweetness in this drink comes from dark maple syrup is a surprise to no one who knows me. So frequently people hear "sprits" or "sparkling" and they automatically think: CHAMPAGNE! But there are so many other options out there. For me, the fall means apples and the harvest and rich fall flavors, so, here, I opted for a sparkling cider. I recommend asking your local wine shop for a very dry and crisp one—nothing too funky. Paired with applejack and nutmeg, this light and peppy falltime sipper is what you'll want to kick off every Thanksgiving from here on out.

HOW TO MAKE THE DRINK

Add all the ingredients, except the cider, to a cocktail shaker filled with ice. Shake and strain into a chilled coupe and top with the cider. Garnish with the apple fan and lemon twist, if using, and serve.

DEALER'S
CHOICE

You just got the bar
job of your dreams.
What celebratory
drink will you make
yourself?

LAND AMONG THE STARS

CREATOR

CHRISTINA MERCADO
Speed Rack competitor

3 ounces (90 ml) sparkling wine

1½ ounces (45 ml) Cognac V.S.

½ ounce (15 ml) Winter Citrus Juice Blend (recipe follows)

½ ounce (15 ml) Winter Citrus Syrup (recipe follows)

Lemon twist, for garnish

For Christina Mercado, her interest in Speed Rack went beyond the built-in community—her mom had breast cancer. "It's something that's always on my mind," she said. "And to see a program consistently dedicated to supporting and talking about the cause is encouraging." When it came to creating this drink, Christina said, "I first began to think about the moment: 'Bar job of your dreams' . . . I began to picture that moment in my mind . . . and when that image became complete, I had a very specific style of drink in my hand. Bubbles, strong bubbles." A riff on the French 75, Christina's cocktail (photo on page 63) swaps out basic lemon juice for a winter citrus blend that she makes from fragrant Meyer lemons and pretty-in-pink Cara Cara oranges. Her simple syrup incorporates the peels from these fruits, too, for a clever and sustainable situation. And then, of course, there are bubbles. So many bubbles.

HOW TO MAKE THE DRINK

Add all the ingredients to a chilled champagne flute. Stir gently to combine. Express the lemon twist over the drink and place it in the glass; serve.

Winter Citrus Syrup and Juice Blend

Makes about 1 ½ cups (360 ml) syrup and 9 ounces (270 ml) juice

3 Meyer lemons, peeled

3 Cara Cara oranges, peeled

1 ounce (30 ml) lemon juice

1 cup (200 g) cane sugar

Peel and juice the Meyer lemons and oranges, keeping the peels separate from the juice.

Combine the Meyer lemon and orange juices with the lemon juice and stir. Store in an airtight container the refrigerator until ready to use; it will keep for about 3 days.

Combine the Meyer lemon and orange peels with the sugar in an airtight container. Mix well, cover, and refrigerate overnight.

Then add the citrus sugar mixture and 7 ounces (210 ml) water to a small pot and place over medium heat. Simmer

for 5 minutes and then remove from the heat. Strain and let cool to room temperature. Store in an airtight container in the refrigerator for up to 1 month. Any extra syrup you have on hand will make a lovely addition to a whiskey or pisco sour.

DEALER'S CHOICE

———

Your best friend is getting married and you're making the drink; give us a liquid round of applause to match the moment.

CREATOR

JORDIE HO-SHUE
Speed Rack competitor

1 ounce (30 ml) London Dry gin

1 ounce (30 ml) Giffard Lichi-Li liqueur

½ ounce (15 ml) Campari

½ ounce (15 ml) Mommenpop Seville Orange aperitif

½ ounce (15 ml) lemon juice

2 ounces (60 ml) prosecco, to top

HERE'S TO YOU!

In addition to being an incredibly talented bartender, Jordie is a DJ and runs her own events business, called Honeyfest, which works to increase representation of female-identifying and other marginalized people in electronic music. "I was drawn into Speed Rack by the tangible impact I saw it have on women's lives," she told us, "And I was extremely attracted to the sense of camaraderie I saw competitors build throughout each season. It had a direct impact on the development of my company." Named for one of her favorite disco songs, this tropical take on the classic daisy template, swapping prosecco for the standard soda water, is certainly deserving of the dance floor. "It's a sparkling cocktail that reeks celebration," she said. Here she pairs gin with fragrant lychee liqueur and lemon juice (a combination she loves) and then bridges these flavors with the bitterness of Campari and woman-owned Mommenpop Seville Orange, a lively, juicy vermouth from California. Here's to you!

HOW TO MAKE THE DRINK

Add all the ingredients, except the prosecco, to a cocktail shaker filled with ice. Shake until cold and double strain into a rocks glass over one large ice cube. Top with the prosecco and serve.

FROM TOP TO BOTTOM:
Here's to You! (page 62),
Land Among the Stars (page 61)

CREATOR

CHRISTINA VEIRA
Speed Rack competitor and coordinator

1½ ounces (45 ml) blanco tequila

½ ounce (15 ml) Cherry Shrub (recipe follows)

½ ounce (15 ml) Gentian liqueur, such as Suze or Bonal

¼ ounce (7.5 ml) lemon juice

3 ounces (90 ml) sparkling wine

SOFT LAUNCH

"To me, hospitality, as an industry, is at its best when it is community- and connection-driven. A large part of that is how we use our influence not only to make our bars better but our broader society better," says Christina Veira. Our community has certainly been made better with her in it. Christina competed once in Toronto, but after that took on the role of our coordinator in Canada. She's an exceptional mentor, someone we consistently look to. And lucky for us, she loves to make bright, playful, stirred drinks, just what this Dealer's Choice called for. For Soft Launch, a sparkling cocktail that's perfect in the hot summer months, Christina makes a ruby-red, tangy cherry shrub. The process takes about four days, so start on a Monday to be weekend-ready. Add any leftovers to seltzer water to make a non-alcoholic sipper once the next week arrives.

HOW TO MAKE THE DRINK

Add all the ingredients, except the sparkling wine, to a mixing glass filled with ice. Stir until cold and strain into a wine glass. Top with the sparkling wine and serve.

Cherry Shrub   *Makes about 4 cups (960 ml)*

---

2 cups (310 g) fresh, pitted cherries

2 cups (420 g) demerara sugar

2 cups (480 ml) high-quality champagne vinegar

Combine the cherries and sugar in a large airtight container. Mix well, crunching up the sugar with a spoon. Place in the refrigerator and allow to macerate for 12 hours, stirring once every 6 hours. Add the vinegar and stir well. Return to the refrigerator and allow to further macerate for 4 days, stirring once a day. Strain through a fine-mesh sieve, pressing the cherries to extract all the liquid. Store in an airtight container in the refrigerator for up to one month.

BICICLETTA #2

CREATOR

KATE BOUSHEL
Speed Rack competitor and coordinator

––––

1 ounce (30 ml) Lillet Blanc

¾ ounce (22.5 ml) Aperol

¼ ounce (7.5 ml) gin

1 dash Bittered Sling Lem-Marrakech bitters

2 ounces (60 ml) cava, to top

Orange twist and a fresh pansy, if in season, or a dried rosebud if not, for garnish

"My dear friend Rehana was diagnosed with breast cancer when she was only twenty-three. She fought valiantly, but in 2012, it came back with a vengeance, and she lost the war against the disease in February 2013, at the age of thirty-one," Kate Boushel told us. "So when I heard about a speed bartending competition that was all about fostering a stronger female bartending community while funding breast cancer research, I was all in." Kate competed in two seasons of Speed Rack Canada and then became our lead organizer for Quebec. "Since 2018, it has become even more important to me as two of my best friends have since been diagnosed with the beast in their late thirties and early forties. So yeah, FUCK CANCER!" We couldn't agree more with her. This cocktail prompt was an ideal one for Kate, as the Negroni Sbagliato (that is, a Negroni that swaps sparkling wine for the gin, page 258) is one of her favorites. And she emphatically takes a no-holds-barred approach to heaping on the ice when it comes to this drink. "The more the better," she said. Whereas most sbagliati are simply just red bitter aperitivo with sweet vermouth and sparkling wine, for her version, Kate adds just ¼ ounce (7.5 ml) of a complex, floral gin (such as Hendrick's Mid-summer Solstice or Del Professore's Monsieur)—an aromatic call and response to the drink's Negroni roots. And, in a citrusy, spicy shout out to Lauren Mote, the woman who first brought Speed Rack to Canada, a dash of Lem-Marrakech bitters from her company, Bittered Sling.

HOW TO MAKE THE DRINK

Add all the ingredients, except the cava, to a rocks glass filled with ice. Stir to integrate, add more fresh ice, and top with the cava. Give a quick stir, express the orange twist over the drink, and place it in the glass. Garnish with the flower and serve.

DEALER'S CHOICE

It's New Year's Eve and we're so ready for the next year. Can you give us a celebratory cocktail that's sparkling with sake or sparkling sake?

CREATOR

LYDIA MCLUEN
Speed Rack competitor, regional winner

---

3 Granny Smith apple slices

1 teaspoon Fennel Syrup (recipe follows)

⅛ teaspoon Ginger Syrup (page 260)

½ ounce (15 ml) vodka, preferably Timberline

½ ounce (15 ml) aquavit, preferably Krogstad

1 teaspoon lemon juice

2 ounces (60 ml) sparkling junmai daiginjo sake, preferably Uka Organic

Slice of candied ginger on a pick, for garnish

PLACE SETTING

The self-described Rocky Balboa of Speed Rack training, Lydia McLuen wasn't about to go to the corner after not making it past prelims in Season 6. She ran the proverbial stairs: "I pored over books to see different specs for drinks like the Cosmopolitan or the Bensonhurst. I studied YouTube videos of previous competitions. When I was given the set of possible drinks for Season 7, I figured out how many total combinations were possible, and laid out careful maps of exactly where I would place each bottle and arrows laying out the steps," she told us. She left Season 7 as the Northwest regional champion. "That day had an astounding impact on my career. In the immediate aftermath, I was hired at a fancy new bar and finally awarded the Friday shift. I had proven I was fast enough." To show off her chops for this book, Lydia made a New Year's drink based in Uka Organic sparkling sake with notes of fennel, apple, and anise. She paired this with a couple spirits from the Pacific Northwest (she's based in Portland, Oregon), as well as fennel and ginger syrups to make a decidedly cold weather, low-ABV sparkler. Yo, Lydia, you did it!

HOW TO MAKE THE DRINK

Add the apple slices and fennel and ginger syrups to a mixing glass. Muddle well to break down the apple slices. Add the vodka, aquavit, and lemon juice. Fill the mixing glass with ice and stir until cold. Add the sparkling sake and stir just to incorporate. Fine strain into a chilled Nick & Nora glass and garnish with the candied ginger on a pick. Serve.

Fennel Syrup

1 medium fennel bulb

1 cup (200 g) granulated sugar

Chop the fennel (including the stems) into manageable pieces and press through an extractor-style juicer. Add 1 cup (240 ml) of the fennel juice and the sugar to a blender pitcher and blend until the sugar is fully dissolved. Pour the syrup into an airtight container and store in the refrigerator for up to 2 weeks. (Any extra fennel juice will be delicious mixed with fresh celery, apple, and lemon juice for a great no-alc, hydrating sipper.)

DEALER'S
CHOICE

Give us a bubbly
cocktail that's made
with tea, something
that celebrates
friendships around
the world.

FAR FROM MUMBAI

For years, Ezra Star stole the spotlight of the Boston bar scene from behind the now-famous bar at Drink. It was named World's Best Bar in the 2013 Spirited Awards, in large part thanks to Ezra's work. Boston has always had a surprising number of outstanding bartenders, but we know she left a big hole when she moved to China a few years back. Today she can be found slinging drinks at Call Me Al, a cocktail bar she runs with her wife (and Speed Rack alum) Beckaly Franks (see page 164). Whereas most French 75s are served without ice, in a flute glass, Ezra prefers hers as a Collins (her favorite drink style) poured tall and over ice, which takes the drink to a new place of refreshment. "I made this drink for a friend from Mumbai who was living in South Africa and missing home," she told us. This drink began with a classic French 75 build (see page 255) and incorporates other ingredients, like strawberries and rooibos tea, that her friend really loves. This is such an ideal warm-weather sipper, from China to South Africa to Mumbai with love.

CREATOR

EZRA STAR
Speed Rack competitor

1 ounce (30 ml) London Dry gin, preferably Bombay Sapphire

½ ounce (15 ml) St-Germain elderflower liqueur

½ ounce (15 ml) Strawberry Syrup (recipe follows)

½ ounce (15 ml) Rooibos Syrup (recipe follows)

½ ounce (15 ml) lemon juice

3 ounces (180 ml) dry sparkling wine, to top

Little yellow edible flowers, for garnish

HOW TO MAKE THE DRINK

Add all the ingredients, except the sparkling wine, to a cocktail shaker filled with ice. Shake to integrate. Double strain into a Collins glass filled with ice and top with the sparkling wine; serve with the edible flower garnish.

Strawberry Syrup
Makes about 2½ cups (600 ml)

1 cup (165 g) strawberries, destemmed and finely chopped

1 cup (195 g) superfine white sugar

¼ teaspoon salt

Add the strawberries, sugar, and salt to a large airtight container. Cover and shake to evenly coat the fruit. Let sit in the refrigerator overnight. Then add 1 cup (240 ml) water and stir to dissolve the sugar. Strain through a fine-mesh strainer and discard the solids. Store in the refrigerator for up to 2 weeks.

Rooibos Syrup
Makes about 1½ cups (360 ml)

2 rooibos tea bags

1 cup (240 ml) hot water

1 cup (200 g) granulated sugar

Combine the tea bags and hot water in an airtight container. Remove the tea bags and while the tea is still hot pour in the sugar. Stir to fully dissolve. Store in the refrigerator for up to 2 weeks.

FROM THE
FOUNDERS

Make this for brunch
parties, premieres,
galas, and breast
cancer benefits.

A PINK AGENDA

CREATOR

**LYNNETTE
MARRERO**
Speed Rack co-founder

1½ ounces (60 ml) pisco,
preferably Peruvian pisco
or Bolivian singani

½ ounce (22.5 ml) lemon
juice

½ ounce (15 ml) grapefruit
juice

¾ ounce (22.5 ml)
Raspberry Syrup (page 261)

3 ounces (90 ml) sparkling
rosé wine, to top

Pinch of salt or dash of
Saline Solution (page 262)

Raspberry, for garnish

This cocktail is an homage to one of our favorite charities, the Pink
Agenda, which raises money for breast cancer research and care. I
created this drink for its annual gala, looking to make something pink
that reflected the smart and sophisticated women who run the organization—and the positive, celebratory occasion. It's a combination of
two old-school drinks: the Paloma (which features tequila and grapefruit, page 257) and the Clover Club (which has gin and raspberry, page
255). In choosing a base, I looked for a similarly aromatic spirit, which
landed me in the zone of grape brandies from South America—either
pisco or singani—both of which have a floral edge that aligns well with
the fruitiness of the drink. The secret sauce? A little pinch of salt or
dash of saline solution that acts as a highlighter for flavor, making for a
lively, vibrant sip.

HOW TO MAKE THE DRINK

Add all the ingredients except the sparkling wine, to a cocktail shaker
filled with ice. Shake until cold and strain into a small wine glass or coupe.
Top with the sparkling wine, garnish with the raspberry, and serve.

CREATOR

CARI HAH
Speed Rack competitor

---

2 fresh shiso leaves

1½ ounces (45 ml) white rum

½ ounce (15 ml) Simple Syrup (page 262)

½ ounce (15 ml) yuzu juice

2 dashes Miracle Mile yuzu bitters (see Resources, page 259)

1 heaping teaspoon Ume Caviar (page 262)

2 to 3 ounces (60 to 90 ml) sparkling wine

Pickled umeboshi plum, on a pick, for garnish (optional)

POPPING PLUMS

The impact Cari Hah has made in the Los Angeles cocktail world is monumental. She has taken numerous up-and-comers under her wing, mentoring, training, and cheering them on to big wins at Speed Rack. She's a big reason the community in LA is so tight. And frankly, her approach to cocktails is just so much fun. "The roots of this drink are the Old Cuban [page 257], just with a bit of my heritage and whimsy," Cari Hah told us. She's taken this modern classic (itself a royale-d mojito) and expanded on it with Japanese flavors of grassy shiso, tangy yuzu citrus, and little bubbles of umeshu, a plum liqueur. "In Asian culture a 'popping' sensation in your mouth is considered a highly pleasant and fun experience. Think ikura salmon roe or the texture of boba pearls. Bubbles are always fun and festive." It's her playful version of Champagne and caviar. If making your own ume caviar sounds daunting, don't worry; assemble a few ingredients (see Resources page 259) and the chemistry is easy and can be applied to any liqueur. Alternatively, you can order both boozy and non-boozy cocktail bubbles online. We recommend the non-alcoholic yuzu ones from Sphera for this drink.

HOW TO MAKE THE DRINK

Muddle the shiso leaves in a cocktail shaker. Fill the shaker with ice and add the rum, simple syrup, yuzu juice, and bitters. Shake until cold and fine strain into a chilled coupe or champagne flute. Add the ume caviar and top the drink with the sparkling wine. Garnish with the umeboshi plum, if desired, and serve.

PUNCH IT UP
How to Scale and Batch Cocktails for a Crowd

We aren't exaggerating when we say that punch plays a massive role in Speed Rack. While the competitors are fretting in the wings between rounds, the hundreds and hundreds of spectators are busying themselves with punch, gallons and gallons of punch. (We love you, sponsors!)

To witness the choreography behind concocting these batches of thousands of cocktails is as good as any ballet we've ever seen. Led by bartenders we've named "batch masters," our faithful volunteers run the punch show, juicing and measuring and mixing mass quantities of punch for the thirsty people, ensuring that what's consumed by the audience is just as well-made and tasty as anything served to judges on the stage. We've seen everything from Chartreuse ice luges to fountains of Fernet and Ford's Gin.

A punch is the ultimate party trick. It's low-lift and it helps keep you, the host, out of the kitchen or from behind the bar so that you can easily entertain. Plus, punches tend to be lower in proof, which will keep your guests from getting twisted on full-proof cocktails before dinner. They're simple, elongated drinks. We love this little punch recipe rhyme that originated in the Caribbean: "one of sour, two of sweet, three of strong, four of weak." They're made with citrus, sugar, spirit, and water of some sort.

Although most contain citrus juice, punches are the exception to the rule; they're meant to be stirred rather than shaken. Shaken drinks can't sit around for long; punches, by definition, have to. Since there will not be any dilution from shaking in ice, it's crucial to add water. We've all bumped into a punch that was just way too syrupy; it was missing its water. We recommend mixing up your punch base in quart-size containers so that you can add them to the bowl and top with sparkling water or wine, then replenish throughout the evening so that the drink doesn't go flat.

Not all batched drinks have to be served in a punch bowl with a pretty ice ring. Essentially, any cocktail can be batched and kept chilled in the freezer or fridge (we love having martinis and Negronis in the freezer for impromptu drinking). Proper dilution will be different for different styles of drinks; for example, a stirred drink made mostly of spirit will require more water than a shaken drink that's royale-d with Champagne. Follow our handy "Diluting Batches" chart below to know how much water to add in.

Another pitfall of punches is figuring out the proper additions of ingredients like bitters, absinthe, or salt, ingredients that are easily controlled in small doses (dashes, rinses, and pinches) but can do wacky things when stirred in in any substantial amount. The beauty of bitters,

DILUTING BATCHES

> **Here's a handy guide to how much water you need to add to each of your batches.**

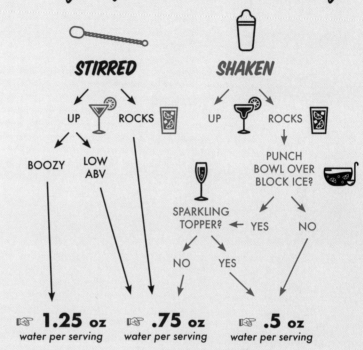

What Style of Drink Are You Making?

STIRRED

SHAKEN

UP → ROCKS

UP ← ROCKS

BOOZY   LOW ABV

PUNCH BOWL OVER BLOCK ICE?

SPARKLING TOPPER? ← YES   NO

NO   YES

☞ **1.25 oz**
water per serving

☞ **.75 oz**
water per serving

☞ **.5 oz**
water per serving

for example, is that they expand when combined with fizzy things, but their intensity can be sort of unpredictable. So, too, the way we measure these good things in small packages isn't all that precise. My dash could be very different from yours. For this reason, we encourage you to convert dashes to ounces for a batch, and to wait to add them until the last minute. For stirred freezer-style batch cocktails like a martini or Manhattan, this means adding bitters to each serving à la minute. For sour-style batches, this means adding the bitters when you'd add the citrus.

5 dashes = ⅛ ounce/3.5 ml (¾ teaspoon)
10 dashes = ¼ ounce/7.5 ml (1½ teaspoons)
20 dashes = ½ ounce/15 ml (1 tablespoon)
30 dashes = ¾ ounce/22.5 ml (1½ tablespoons)

For a batch that calls for 40 dashes or more, we recommend multiplying the number of dashes by 0.028 to get the yield of bitters in ounces. This multiplier takes into account the increased potency of bitters when they're in higher volumes. So, for 40 dashes of bitters, use 1.12 ounces of bitters (1 ounce plus ¾ teaspoon).

Lacy Hawkins with her Aura Frame (page 82) to match

CHAPTER 3

IT'S A LONG GAME

HIGHBALLS, COLLINSES, AND OTHER LONG FIZZY SIPPERS

This category of lanky, effervescent drinks is a go-to for many people who create cocktails for a living; they're usually incredibly refreshing, pretty simple, entirely satisfying, and all with a relatively low ABV. It's where many minds tend to go when creating a drink for someone who isn't sure what they want; the sparkling elongation somehow makes these cocktails more approachable. There's a reason this is one of the longer chapters in the book!

The name of the game with this genre of built cocktails (that is, drinks that are "built" in the glass, as opposed to being shaken or stirred) is to lengthen and enliven a spirit with something bracingly bubbly, and in the case of a Collins or fizz, to stretch out the sour's classic spirit to citrus to sweetener ratio. Slightly more advanced than a rum and Coke or gin & tonic, these tall, fizzy blank canvases are an opportunity to show off your creativity, be it with signature syrups, interesting spirit combinations, or solitary spears of ice. Commit to memory a few of these tall templates and you'll be well on your way.

The Fizz Family Tree

The most simplistic of this category of drinks is the highball. There's something very rewarding in casually introducing a spirit to soda. And there's no shame in its ease. A lot of what we do as bartenders is make some sort of flavorful syrup and add fresh juice and booze. But a soda, be it tonic or ginger beer or grapefruit soda, is also just that: a balance of sweet and tart to mix with your spirit of choice. Today companies like Fever-Tree, London Essence, and Betty Buzz are in the business of making mixers specifically tailored to cocktails and spirits. They've done all the work of getting the acid and the sugar and the flavor correct for you. All you have to do is add booze—around 2 ounces (60 ml)—for a tasty highball. If you're feeling slightly more ambitious, make your own soda blend, as Ivy has with her Wise Up (page 93). The potential for using the highball blueprint as a springboard for a more complex cocktail is infinite: Add a couple dashes of celery or mole bitters; split your base spirit between blanco tequila and pisco or devise a blend of rums; whip up a spicy pineapple syrup; or embellish the drink with an over-the-top bouquet of herbs.

Mules and bucks are their own subsets of highballs, both of which involve ginger in some form. The line between the two drinks is a little blurry, but by definition, a buck is composed of a spirit, citrus, and ginger, whereas a mule can be as low-lift as vodka mixed with ginger beer. There are numerous variations of bucks and mules that have emerged as modern classics; the Gin-Gin Mule, devised by Audrey Saunders, begins with her homemade ginger beer and brings gin and

muddled mint (a nod to a mojito) to the equation. Here, Lacy Hawkins fizzes up a mule with a lager in her Aura Frame (page 82) and Mony Bunni adds extra spice to her bourbon buck with a Ceylon tea–based syrup (page 90).

As for the Collins template, it's a sour served over ice, elongated with something carbonated to make it even more refreshing, and generally served in a 12 ounce (360 ml) glass. This could be soda water, a split of soda and sparkling wine, or even beer. The classic sour recipe is 2:¾:¾, spirit:citrus:sweetener, shaken, but you can certainly take liberties there, 2:1:1, say, if you're going for something that's a little less spirit forward. And there's room to veer off the equal parts of your sour ratio with more citrus or more sweetener, depending on the type of citrus you're using (and the season) or concentration of sugar in your syrup, be it a standard 1:1 simple syrup or a rich 2:1 simple or a 2:1 honey syrup, for example.

Then there's the fizz—basically the Collins's little sister. Put your sour base in a shorter rocks glass—8 ounces (240 ml) will do—and fill it up with chilled soda water, no ice. To give it some froth, add in an egg white or aquafaba, for our vegan friends. We love Carley Noel Hansen's Fizzness as Usual (page 85), which combines rye whiskey, Montenegro amaro, and pineapple gum for a fluffy, tall tropical drink.

Sizing Up Your Glass

While seemingly easy to make, the challenge of these elongated drinks is finding proper balance. There's nowhere to hide with these cocktails. Begin with a tall, skinny glass. Many fancy cocktail bars will have both highball glasses (around 10 ounces [300 ml]) and Collins glasses (around 12 ounces [360 ml]) But for the home bartender, glassware styles come and go. if you have a super-size glass, you'll want to scale up the drink accordingly. Think of it this way: Say you're making a gin & tonic, and you only have a teacup or a pint glass. If you put the same amount of gin in both of those vessels and top them up with tonic, you're going to end up with one very strong drink and one very weak one. You'll need to adjust your proportions to fit the glass.

Find Your Chill

Not only is the glass a factor in the volume of your drink but so is your ice. All ice may be "just frozen water," but not all ice is created equal. Many, many bartenders can talk endlessly on the merits of good ice, but we will spare you. Here's what you should know: that perfectly chiseled, clear ice rock in a drink at your favorite cocktail bar is far different from what comes plunking out of your freezer. If you have crappy ice, odds are the drink will be too watery and not all that cold. See page 21 for how to make nice ice at home.

All About Bubbles

Then, of course, there are the bubbles! At this point there are rows and rows of sparkling water options and umpteen flavored sodas in every grocery and deli. If you want to geek out on tonic, feel free, just be sure to taste whatever you buy before using it, so that you can make adjustments as needed. For example, some ginger beers have a lot of citrus flavor and others are particularly earthy. There's plenty of variation in basic soda water, too. Each will have different sized bubbles, and some will be saltier than others. Knowing where you're starting will make for a much better drink in the end. And no matter what, make sure your soda's nice and cold before you start.

Your objective, above all, is to integrate the bubbles all the way through the cocktail. The last thing you want is to have a drink taste like plain soda water for the first few sips and finish with a sweet-tart puddle of citrus in the bottom. How best to achieve this is up to you, be it pouring the soda first and allowing the other ingredients to incorporate naturally as you build the drink or to gently stir the final cocktail before serving.

Here, we present a dozen diverse and statuesque cocktails that range from fruity and cloudlike to outrageously mouthwatering and pickle-y so that you might navigate the bubbly continuum.

DEALER'S CHOICE

———

Make us a mule that celebrates the spices and flavors from your travels around the world.

AURA FRAME

CREATOR

LACY HAWKINS
Speed Rack competitor, regional and USA national winner

———

Tajín, for garnish

1¼ ounces (37.5 ml) blended scotch whiskey, preferably Johnnie Walker Black Label

1 ounce (30 ml) Chinola passion fruit liqueur

½ ounce (15 ml) lime juice

½ ounce (15 ml) Ginger Syrup (page 260)

3 ounces (90 ml) light lager, such as Presidente, to top

Lime wheel, for garnish

To watch Lacy Hawkins compete in Speed Rack was to witness pure, unadulterated determination. We'd never seen anything like it. When she first took the stage in Portland, Oregon, bringing a whole entourage of friends and fans with her, she was very new to the industry, and she just kept coming back, persevering until, in her fifth season, she won the whole thing. Since then she's gone on to bartend at some of the best bars in the US, including New York City's Clover Club and the Nomad. "Speed Rack connected me to people and opportunities that I never would have known were available. It opened doors and gave me a platform to establish myself within the beverage industry," she says. Her style is irreverent and approachable. "I like juicy, delicious, chuggable drinks," she says—and the Aura Frame (photo on page 78) is just that. She started by mulling over ginger beer as a highball ingredient and wound up thinking about ginger . . . and beer. "Why not make a shandy with ginger syrup, smoky scotch, and some beer?" she asks. With a rim of tangy, spicy Tajín seasoning and toss-back-friendly pilsner, this is a total pleaser of a drink, one that Lacy recommends batching out and serving at parties or even making into a punch (see page 76).

HOW TO MAKE THE DRINK

Rim a Collins glass with Tajín and fill it with ice. Add all the ingredients, except the beer, to a cocktail shaker filled with ice. Give a quick shake and strain into the glass. Top with the beer, garnish with the lime wheel, and serve.

WHAT'S YOUR GO-TO DRINK STYLE?

"The spritz. It's full of potential."
—NATASHA DAVID

"I love to make spirit-only cocktails. It's easy to throw a fruit juice and a syrup together and make a crushable drink, but there's a level of skill and cocktail complexity that is required to achieve the same thing with spirit-only cocktails."
—J'NAI ANGELLE

"Sweet, dessert-style cocktails— the kind I enjoy drinking. My ethos is that cocktails are a treat. They tend to have no nutritional value and the same caloric content as a McDonald's cheeseburger, so they should be enjoyed as such."
—MILLIE TANG

"All I do: down hooey but a bit fruity!"
—SIAN BUGHAN

"Stirred, low-ABV. All things vermouth, sherry, and amaro."
—DAPHNEE VARY DESHAIES

"Take your favorite classic cocktail and sub the base spirit for something unexpected. I love to invite folks to explore from within their comforts. Get freaky with some sherry, cognac, or eau de vie. Life's short, try weird shit."
—ELYSE BLECHMAN

"I love developing daisy cocktails. There is so much flexibility to play around with, but I always try to make my cocktails easy to drink and crushable."
—JESS POMERANTZ

"Depends on the day, the weather, and the mood I'm in! Today? I'm feeling built and spritzy."
—MIRANDA BREEDLOVE

"I love highballs. They're incredibly underrated as a cocktail category."
—IRENE KERN

"An equal-parts cocktail. So simple, but hard to come up with at the same time."
—RHACHEL SHAW

"If I want to make something to satisfy the majority I usually go with a sour, but I think making stirred cocktails is a much more fun challenge because you don't have the amount of citrus and sugar to hide behind."
—COLIE EHRENWORTH

"I love to make stirred versions of sour or bubbly drinks. Think deconstructed French 75, or a margarita that is smooth, silky, yet layered and dynamic."
—NATASHA MESA

"Bitter and boozy! I have always half-joked that my favorite style of cocktail is, coincidentally, also my personality."
—HALEY TRAUB

CREATOR

CARLEY NOEL HANSEN

Speed Rack competitor

1 egg white

1½ ounces (45 ml) rye whiskey

½ ounce (15 ml) Montenegro amaro

¾ ounce (22.5 ml) lemon juice

¾ ounce (22.5 ml) pineapple gum (gomme) syrup (see Resources, page 259)

¼ ounce (7.5 ml) Cinnamon Syrup (page 260)

1 ounce (30 ml) soda water, to top

Lemon twist and a brandied cherry, for garnish

FIZZNESS AS USUAL

For years, Carley Noel Hansen and her Chicago-based company H2O1 were crucial in making sure that our midwestern competitions went off without a hitch. She's an excellent bartender in her own right, as evidenced by this nuanced whiskey fizz. A truly old-school cocktail style made of spirit, sugar, citrus, and sparkling water, the fizz has evolved over the last two hundred years, with versions now involving ice, egg yolks or whites, or a whole egg entirely. For this, Carley goes the way of the Silver Fizz, one of the fizzes that employ egg whites, along with lemon and gin. Here, rye whiskey meets bittersweet amaro, lemon, and two syrups: a pineapple gum (gomme) that brings fruitiness and a slinky texture, and a cinnamon syrup that zeros in on the spice in the amaro quite nicely. This drink is a smart go-to for when the occasion calls for a lighter whiskey drink. A word to the wise: Carley recommends cracking the egg white into the shaker before adding anything else—that way, should any yolk or shell land in the tin, it can be fished out before the pricier booze comes into play.

HOW TO MAKE THE DRINK

Add the egg white to a cocktail shaker. Add the rest of the ingredients, except for the soda water, and shake until the egg white is frothy. Fill the shaker with ice and shake until cold. Strain into a Collins glass filled with ice and top with the soda water. Garnish with the lemon twist and cherry, and serve.

PLAN AHEAD

AXE TO RIND

An expert in drinks that take a culinary slant, Clairessa Chaput's cocktails often recall her own taste memories—this Collins does both. "I focused on the briny aspect of this prompt and thought about some of my fave housemade pickles," she told us. "Watermelon rinds were the first thing that came to mind. They are such a tasty way to utilize almost all the melon." Shrubs are a smart way to use up any extra or produce or even scraps and will bring a nice vinegary tartness to drinks—just know that, as with Clairessa's Watermelon Rind Shrub, they can take a couple of days to make. The drink layers on the flavors—salty fino sherry meets floral blanc vermouth meets herbaceous gin meets pickle-y watermelon—topped with soda water to give an intensely refreshing result. And in case you're looking for even more salinity, a cube of feta as a garnish takes the whole thing home.

CREATOR

CLAIRESSA CHAPUT
Speed Rack competitor, regional winner

½ ounce (15 ml) lemon juice

1 ounce (30 ml) Watermelon Rind Shrub (recipe follows)

½ ounce (15 ml) fino sherry

½ ounce (15 ml) blanc vermouth, preferably Dolin

1 ounce (30 ml) gin

4 ounces (120 ml) soda water, to top

Feta cheese cube and watermelon cube on a pick, for garnish

HOW TO MAKE THE DRINK

Add all the ingredients, except the soda water, to a cocktail shaker filled with ice. Shake until cold and strain into a Collins glass over ice. Top with the soda water and give a quick stir. Garnish with the feta and watermelon, and serve.

Watermelon Rind Shrub

Makes about 2 cups (480 ml)

---

12 ounces (340 g) watermelon rind

½ ounce (15 ml) lemon juice

3 ounces (90 ml) apple cider vinegar

⅓ cup (65 g) granulated sugar

Add the watermelon rind, lemon juice, and apple cider vinegar to a blender pitcher and puree. Strain through a fine-mesh strainer and set aside. Combine the sugar and water in a saucepan over low heat and bring to a

boil. Remove from the heat and stir until the sugar is fully dissolved. Add this syrup to the watermelon rind puree and blend again until fully integrated. Pour into an airtight container and skim any foam off

the surface. Store in the refrigerator for at least 2 days before using and up to 1 month.

Give us a refreshing
whiskey cocktail
to sip on a hot
summer day. Think
Bondi Beach with a
surfboard in hand.

EARLY RETIREMENT

CREATOR

MILLIE TANG
Speed Rack competitor,
Australia national
winner

1½ ounces (45 ml) bourbon

¾ ounce (22.5 ml)
Spiced Pineapple Honey
(page 262)

2 dashes black walnut
bitters

3 ounces (90 ml)
carbonated coconut water,
or unsweetened coconut-
flavored sparkling water,
to top

Lemon coin, for garnish

Based in Brisbane, Australia, Millie Tang started as a photographer who moonlighted as a bartender—almost on a whim. Since her early days behind the bar, she's gone on to win a number of competitions, as well as earning the title of Australian Bartender of the Year. She was the winner of our second season in Australia, in November 2019, after being the runner up our first year there. Now she's a bartender who moonlights as a photographer. Millie's drinks style is big flavors in seemingly simple serves, building impressive complexity through ingredients. Her Early Retirement is a personal classic, she told us. This drink had its beginnings as an old-fashioned (page 254) twist. "I thought pineapple would be an interesting addition and it also helped strengthen the boardroom vs. island life concept of the drink," Millie said. It became part of the sweetener for the drink, in the form of a pineapple honey that's spiced with cardamom, cloves, cinnamon, and the elusive (and not all that legal in the USA) tonka bean. "But the plane was too one-dimensional," she said. "It required a lot of height and length to make room for the sticky gold and pearl notes." This sent her in the direction of whiskey highball, and, as she'd always tasted coconut notes in bourbon, carbonated coconut water seemed a natural fit. Millie advises that anyone with a SodaStream, or similar sparkling water maker, has all they need to infuse coconut water with bubbles. Otherwise, just replace it with coconut-flavored sparkling water.

HOW TO MAKE THE DRINK

Add the bourbon, spiced pineapple honey, and bitters to a Collins glass. Add a splash of the carbonated coconut water and stir to combine. Fill the glass with ice and top with more coconut water. Express the lemon coin over the drink, place it in the glass, and serve.

BABA, LET ME TELL YOU ONE THING

CREATOR

MONY BUNNI
Speed Rack competitor, regional and USA national winner

2 ounces (60 ml) bourbon, preferably Four Roses

¾ ounce (22.5 ml) Arabic Tea Syrup (recipe follows)

¾ ounce (22.5 ml) lemon juice

2 dashes Bitter Truth Jerry Thomas Decanter Bitters

2 ounces (60 ml) ginger beer, preferably Fentimans, to top

Star anise pod, for garnish

Here, Mony Bunni heaps even more warming spice notes onto the Mule template, with a fragrant tea syrup that's infused with star anise, cinnamon, cloves, and cardamom. Combining bourbon and ginger beer, the drink is soothing in all the best ways, while being entirely gulpable. The name of this cocktail is a nod to her dad. "For as long as I can remember, my father always started every lecture with the phrase, 'Baba, let me tell you one thing . . .'" Mony recalls. "It became a joke between my sisters and me because, of course, what followed was never 'one thing,' but more like fifty things, and two hours. Even now that we're adults, we still know, every time we hear that phrase, to buckle in for a long ride." While this cocktail is very simple to construct, the syrup does take about a day to infuse, so plan accordingly; a long ride for a long drink.

HOW TO MAKE THE DRINK

Add all the ingredients, except the ginger beer, to a cocktail shaker filled with ice. Shake until cold and strain into a Collins glass over ice. Top with the ginger beer, garnish with the star anise, and serve.

Arabic Tea Syrup

Makes about 1½ cups (360 ml)

2 star anise pods

2 cinnamon sticks

3 whole cloves

5 whole green cardamom pods, lightly crushed

1¼ cups (250 g) granulated sugar

1 cup (240 ml) brewed Ceylon tea

In a skillet over low heat, toast the anise, cinnamon, cloves, and cardamom just until they are fragrant. Add the sugar and tea, increase the heat to medium, and stir until the sugar is dissolved. Pour into an airtight container and let the syrup steep overnight. Strain out the spices and store in the refrigerator for up to 1 month. This syrup also makes a great addition to an old-fashioned or a whiskey sour.

CREATOR

IVY MIX
Speed Rack co-founder

½ ounce (15 ml) Giffard Caribbean Pineapple liqueur

½ ounce (15 ml) Sage Syrup (recipe follows)

½ ounce (15 ml) "Fake Lime" (recipe follows)

1½ ounces (45 ml) clear spirit of choice

2 ounces (60 ml) soda water, to top

Fresh sage leaves, for garnish (optional)

WISE UP

Years ago, while working at my bar Leyenda, bartender Shannon Ponche (see page 40) made a drink called the Lil' Smokey with mezcal, cachaça, pineapple, lime, and sage. Ever since, pineapple and sage has been a favorite combo of mine. I've been really inspired by the cocktail-centric sodas that have been produced in recent years and started experimenting myself. I like to use a blend of acid powders (see Resources, page 259), coined "fake lime" by science-whiz bartender Dave Arnold, rather than using fresh citrus, because it winds up tasting more like "real soda." As added perks, it won't spoil, which means there's no disappointment over crusty old limes in my fruit drawer, and it's super-consistent, which is not always the case with "real lime." My spirit preference here is blanco tequila, but this drink can be a little bit of a choose-your-own-adventure because the soda is delicious with gin, vodka, rum, tequila, and even mezcal. Feel free to tinker with the liqueur/herb combinations, too—grapefruit and rosemary or banana and mint would also be tasty.

HOW TO MAKE THE DRINK

Add all the ingredients, except for the soda water, to a highball glass filled with ice. Top with the soda water and stir well to integrate; garnish with fresh sage, if using; serve.

Sage Syrup   *Makes about 1½ cups (360 ml)*

¼ cup (9 g) fresh sage leaves

1 cup (195 g) superfine sugar

Prepare a small ice bath. Bring a small pot of water to a boil. Reduce to a simmer and submerge the sage leaves in the hot water for about 10 seconds. Remove the leaves from the hot water and immediately dunk in the ice bath. Add the sugar, 1 cup (240 ml) water, and the sage leaves to a blender pitcher. Blend until fully integrated. Fine strain using a chinois, coffee filter, or nut bag into an airtight container. Store in the refrigerator for up to 1 week.

"Fake Lime"   *Makes about 1 cup (240 ml)*

2 tablespoons (18 g) citric acid powder

4 teaspoons (12 g) malic acid powder

6½ tablespoons (25 g) phosphoric acid 1.25% solution

Combine all ingredients with 2 ounces (60 ml) water in a food-safe container. Whisk until dissolved. Store in the refrigerator for up to 2 months.

XOCHIMILCO COLLINS

CREATOR

KAITLYN STEWART
Speed Rack competitor and judge

¾ ounce (22.5 ml) blanco tequila

¾ ounce (22.5 ml) mezcal

½ ounce (15 ml) Aperol

¼ ounce (7.5 ml) Galliano liqueur

¾ ounce (22.5 ml) grapefruit juice

¼ ounce (7.5 ml) lime juice

3 sprigs rosemary (reserve one for garnish)

2½ ounces (75 ml) ginger beer, to top

Grapefruit wheel, for garnish

Kaitlyn Stewart has made a name for herself as a badass competitor not only through Speed Rack, but by winning both the Canadian and global World Class competitions. She's also been a leader in efforts to ensure members of the LGBTQIA community have a place in the global bar scene. Her bartending style is effortless and approachable, and we always learn something from her. Here's her cocktail philosophy: "Play around with your ratios. Find out what works for your palate," says Kaitlyn. For her, that means shaken, citrus-forward cocktails that are light, bright, and refreshing, as with this beachy and tall Paloma. Mexico's signature cocktail is beloved for its unfussiness, but here, "I wanted to take the elements of a Paloma and elevate them," Kaitlyn says. "All while staying true to its roots: agave, citrus, sugar, and a lengthener." To emphasize the agave, she splits the base with tequila and mezcal and then cleverly rounds out the edges of the drink, with Aperol softening the grapefruit, and ginger beer plying the smokiness of the mezcal. Fresh herbs are a great tool for bringing more aromatic character to a cocktail. In this case, rosemary, both shaken in and as a garnish, brings "a touch of earthiness and that 'green' spring note," Kaitlyn says.

HOW TO MAKE THE DRINK

Add the tequila, mezcal, Aperol, Galliano, and grapefruit and lime juices to a cocktail shaker. Place 2 of the rosemary sprigs in between the palms of your hands and roll them back and forth to open up all of the aromatics. Add them to the shaker, fill it with ice, and shake until cold. Fine strain into a Collins glass over fresh ice. Top with the ginger beer and give a quick stir. Garnish with the remaining sprig of rosemary and the grapefruit wheel, and serve.

DEALER'S
CHOICE

New Orleans is dear
to every bartender's
heart, so make us
a tall drink that
screams the Big Easy.

SEAFOOD ON A SATURDAY

CREATOR

J'NAI ANGELLE
Speed Rack competitor

¼ ounce (7.5 ml) agave nectar, plus more for the rim

½ teaspoon Tony Chachere's Creole Seasoning, plus more for the rim

2 ounces (60 ml) reposado tequila

½ ounce (15 ml) Cointreau

½ ounce (15 ml) lemon juice

¼ ounce (7.5 ml) ginger liqueur, preferably Barrow's Intense Ginger Liqueur

1 to 2 dashes Zatarain's Concentrated Shrimp & Crab Boil

2 ounces (60 ml) cream soda, to top

Lemon twist, for garnish

Is it possible to put a city in a glass? J'Nai Angelle proves it is with this drink. Obviously, New Orleans has played an important role as the birthplace of many classic cocktails (including the Sazerac, Vieux Carré, Ramos Gin Fizz, etc.), but when given this prompt, J'Nai, a NOLA native, took a more personal than historical take on the town. "This cocktail is inspired by a joyous Saturday sitting by the Mississippi River eating boiled seafood and drinking an ice-cold cream soda, my favorite pairing," she says. Her drink draws on the template of a Tom Collins (gin, lemon, sugar, and soda) but takes many liberties, swapping in reposado tequila as the base spirit, with agave nectar and ginger liqueur working as sweeteners, and cream soda standing in for soda water for "a creamier texture and flavor." The Collins takes a spiced-up, deeply savory turn with the addition of ingredients found in the pantry of any New Orleans kitchen worth its salt: Creole seasoning and Zatarain's, both of which are widely available in grocery stores. These bring in the peppery, herbal, garlicky spices that perfume the city on lazy weekend afternoons.

HOW TO MAKE THE DRINK

Rim a Collins glass with Creole seasoning by pouring a little agave nectar and a little of the seasoning, separately, on a plate. Dip half of the rim of the glass into the nectar and then into the seasoning. Add all the ingredients, except the cream soda, to a cocktail shaker filled with ice. Shake until cold and then strain into the rimmed glass over fresh ice. Top with the cream soda. Express the lemon twist over the drink, place it in the glass, and serve.

FROM THE
FOUNDERS

Make this for anyone
wanting the little
black dress of
cocktails.

VINTAGE COCO

Vintage Coco hearkens to a woman who knows what she wants. It's a drink I created for women's history month in which I wanted to evoke the idea of powerful, fashionable, elegant, and international women. This is a drink for someone who you might find having a drink at the hotel bar after shopping at the most upscale boutiques in Paris or Singapore. I based this cocktail in blended scotch, an intense and robust but balanced spirit that has a fruitier profile, with a very mild smokiness. And then I started adding to it with tropical flavors like coconut and pineapple, shiso and tangy lime and yuzu soda.

HOW TO MAKE THE DRINK

Add the coconut water, pineapple juice, and scotch to a highball glass filled with ice cubes. Add the soda and gently stir to mix. Garnish with a shiso leaf or mint sprig and serve.

CREATOR

LYNNETTE
MARRERO
Speed Rack co-founder

2 ounces (60 ml) coconut water

½ ounce (15 ml) pineapple juice

1½ ounces (45 ml) blended scotch

2 ounces (60 ml) Fever-Tree Sparkling Lime & Yuzu

Shiso leaf or mint sprig, for garnish

Give us a refreshing, bright drink that we would sip on a beautiful spring day in Kentucky.

CREATOR

ANGEL TETA
Speed Rack competitor, regional winner

1½ ounces (45 ml) bourbon, preferably Angel's Envy Finished in Port Wine Barrels

¾ ounce (22.5 ml) Raspberry Syrup (page 261)

½ ounce (15 ml) lime juice

2½ ounces (75 ml) Fever-Tree Sparkling Pink Grapefruit soda, to top (see Resources, page 259)

Grapefruit twist and/or fresh raspberries, for garnish

THE SLOW WINK

Angel Teta has done *alllll* the things when it comes to Speed Rack. She competed in three seasons—and even won in 2015 in Seattle—and now like many alumni, she's a mentor for our younger upstarts. She's the sort of person you want on your team and she's a thoughtful bartender, to boot. For this Dealer's Choice, Angel had a whiskey-based highball in mind, and looked to a little-known classic, The Blinker, for inspiration. The drink dates back to the 1930s, first appearing in print in Patrick Gavin Duffy's 1934 *The Official Mixer's Manual*, with a call for rye whiskey, grapefruit juice, and grenadine. Today, most bartenders swap raspberry syrup for the grenadine, following the lead of cocktail historian Ted Haigh. Here, Angel pushes it even further into the current era. "I wanted to take a favorite and 'modernize' it a bit," she says. So, she elongated the drink with bubbles, replacing the grapefruit juice with grapefruit soda, and perked it up with some lime juice and her own homemade raspberry syrup. We'll follow her lead.

HOW TO MAKE THE DRINK

Add all the ingredients except the grapefruit soda to a cocktail shaker filled with ice. Shake until cold and strain into a highball glass filled with ice. Top with the grapefruit soda and garnish with a grapefruit twist and/or a fresh raspberry or two. Serve.

CREATOR

MARISELA
DOBSON
Speed Rack competitor

¾ ounce (22.5 ml) London Dry gin, preferably Beefeater

¾ ounce (22.5 ml) genever, preferably Bols

¾ ounce (22.5 ml) UME plum liqueur

¾ ounce (22.5 ml) lemon juice

¼ ounce (7.5 ml) Demerara Syrup (page 260)

2 dashes orange bitters

1 teaspoon edible glitter (see Resources, page 259)

3 ounces (90 ml) tonic water, to top

Lemon twist, for garnish

SOFT GIRL ERA

When Marisela Dobson went to watch Speed Rack in New York City back in 2014, she hadn't even considered bartending as a career path. "Being in the room with such high energy, love, and support I knew I wanted to try it at some point." Five years later, and with three years of bartending under her belt, she competed in Season 9. Today this small package of energy and strength holds down the bar at Brooklyn's Jupiter Disco. When faced with this prompt, she knew exactly what she wanted to do: an elevated gin-and-tonic-meets sour. "I love making sours," she told us. "This is equally balanced with sugar and citrus, with a split base of spirits for multiple layers of flowers, herbs, and citrus." The result is something that she thinks of as somewhat of a self-portrait in cocktail form. "'Soft Girl Era,' she's sparkling and vibrant on the eyes—like me. This drink represents my softer side: light, subtly complex, yet still fun."

HOW TO MAKE THE DRINK

Add all the ingredients, except the tonic water, to a Collins glass filled with ice. Stir to incorporate and top with the tonic water. Express the lemon twist over the drink and place it in the glass. Serve.

CREATOR

SYLVI ROY
Speed Rack competitor, regional winner

———

1½ ounces (45 ml) gin, preferably Hardcore

¾ ounce (22.5 ml) Hibiscus Tea Syrup (recipe follows)

½ ounce (15 ml) lemon juice

1 egg white

2 to 3 ounces (60 to 90 ml) soda water, to top

Edible flowers, such as viola or cornflower, and a lemon wheel, for garnish

HEARTBEATS FIZZ

We heart Sylvi Roy's sweet-tart, hot pink Heartbeats Fizz. And we adore that egg whites are her love language. "When being asked for something that exudes love, I immediately thought of an egg white sour, which is a bright, delicious crowd-pleaser that is very easy to modify with ingredients you can snag from a grocery store," she says. Growing up, Sylvi's dad showed her a whole world of flavor through his cooking, and she's brought much of what he taught her into her bartending, building on the spirit as the "protein" with other flavors that will complement it. For this, she started with a forwardly floral gin (she likes Hardcore gin, made in her hometown of Portland, Maine) and paired it with an easy-to-make hibiscus tea syrup. "Don't be afraid of egg whites!" says Sylvi. "They add a silky texture to the liquid and fluffy foam on top that takes on the other flavors." Here, she first shakes the cocktail with ice and then strains it and re-shakes it sans ice, for more aeration and froth, then serves without ice as is classic in the fizz template. Sylvi names many drinks with song titles; this one's named for José Gonzalez's "Heartbeats," a song that always reminds her of her dad.

HOW TO MAKE THE DRINK

Add all the ingredients, except the soda water, to a cocktail shaker filled with ice. Shake until cold and strain the mixture back into the shaker without ice. Shake until frothy and pour into a Collins glass. Top with the soda water, garnish with the flowers and lemon wheel, and serve.

Hibiscus Tea Syrup

Makes about 1½ cups (360 ml)

3 hibiscus tea bags (3 tablespoons, if using loose tea)

1 cup (200 g) granulated sugar

Boil 1 cup (240 ml) water and pour it over the tea bags in a heat-safe container with a lid. Let steep for 5 minutes. Remove the tea bags and, while the tea is still hot, stir in the sugar until fully dissolved. Let cool to room temperature and store in the refrigerator for up to 1 month.

HOW TO STOCK YOUR BAR

For Speed Rack competitions, we keep a pretty well-edited and streamlined (though admittedly wobbly) bar, but even so it's a lot of bottles. Building a home bar can be daunting considering how vast liquor stores are at this point. But taking the time to meditate on the way you drink and the sorts of cocktails you like is useful when stocking your bar with bottles you'll actually use.

Bitters, syrups, and sodas aside, to achieve your ideal 10- or 12-bottle bar, you'll want to keep bottles from each of these three categories on hand:

BASE SPIRITS

If you adore bourbon, a bar full of gin won't serve you very well. We've already established that a great way to experiment with cocktails is to replace spirits with other ones in classic recipes. This is most easily achieved by swapping spirits that share a common ground. We often think of spirits in "families" of sorts. Aim to have three or four from your preferred family. Which drinking profile fits you best?

I like bourbon: Obviously, other whiskeys (rye, scotch, etc.) come to mind, but there's more to the barrel-aged spirit category. Try a European brandy, such as cognac or Spanish brandy, or venture into the realm of reposado and añejo tequilas. Similarly, an aged rum could do you well.

I like gin: Then you're in the zone of flavorful, clear spirits! There are some obvious relatives, including other botanical spirits like caraway-scented aquavit and Dutch genevers, but you can (and should!) experiment with South American piscos, fruity (but not smoked) agave spirits, and grassy, unaged rhum agricole from Martinique.

I like scotch: Scotch is a broad category (from potent, flavorful blended scotches to super peaty Islay single malts), but one thing is for sure, you certainly like intensity. Other whiskeys to try are rye and Japanese whiskeys.

But other robust spirits such as mezcal, sotol, or Jamaican rum might do the trick, too.

I like tequila: Agave lends itself to rich, fruit-forward flavors, which can also be found in Armagnacs, Calvados, and fruit-based eaux de vie. If it's the earthy aspect you're looking for, try blended Scotch or grassy rhum agricole. On the lower ABV side of things, palo cortado sherry can be a good substitute.

I like vodka: You're looking for some clarity. White rum, with little to no aging, should fit the bill, as will unaged shochu (made from sugar cane). Investigate sake for something lower in proof.

SPIRIT-BASED MODIFIERS

This is a wide-spanning category that encompasses everything from fruit and herbal liqueurs to red bitter aperitivi and many amari. Consider the specific cocktails you love to drink and go from there. If you make margaritas every Friday, you'll need an orange liqueur like Grand Marnier. If Negronis are your thing, then Campari (or something similar like Contratto) will be important. Last Word lovers, be sure to stock up on green Chartreuse. For those who often find themselves in the tropical realm, velvet falernum and allspice dram make sense.

WINE-BASED MODIFIERS

Considering the popularity of sherry and vermouth these days, you could nearly fill your whole bar with these bottles. As with the liqueurs above, what you need from this category will lie in the styles of drinks you make. Martini fans will definitely need some dry vermouth, whereas Manhattan lovers will need sweet. For those who like to drink lower ABV cocktails, sherry in a couple forms, both aged and not, will come in handy, as will Madeira.

If you are a
MARGARITA DRINKER

You always have:

BLANCO OR
REPOSADO TEQUILA

ORANGE LIQUEUR, SUCH AS
COINTREAU

Add these bottles to your bar:

BASE SPIRITS

MEZCAL
COGNAC
GIN
IRISH WHISKEY
VODKA

MODIFIERS

CAMPARI
APEROL
YELLOW CHARTREUSE
MARASCHINO LIQUEUR
APRICOT LIQUEUR

**Now you can also make
these classics:**

AQUEDUCT
BRANDY CRUSTA
CORPSE REVIVER #2
COSMOPOLITAN
GIMLET, GIN OR VODKA

IRISH COCKTAIL
JASMINE
NAKED AND FAMOUS
OAXACA OLD-FASHIONED
PALOMA
SIDECAR
SUFFERING BASTARD

If you are a
MANHATTAN DRINKER

You always have:

RYE WHISKEY
BOURBON
SWEET VERMOUTH
AROMATIC BITTERS

Add these bottles to your bar:

BASE SPIRITS

SCOTCH
IRISH WHISKEY
GIN

MODIFIERS

GREEN CHARTREUSE
DRY VERMOUTH
MARASCHINO LIQUEUR
CAMPARI
BENEDICTINE

FERNET

CYNAR

ORANGE BITTERS

Now you can also make these classics:

BENSONHURST

BOBBY BURNS

BOULEVARDIER

FANCY FREE

MARTINEZ

NEGRONI

PERFECT BQE

ROB ROY

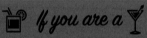 *If you are a*

NEGRONI/MARTINI DRINKER

You always have:

GIN

CAMPARI

SWEET VERMOUTH

DRY VERMOUTH

ORANGE BITTERS

Add these bottles to your bar:

BASE SPIRITS

BOURBON

RYE WHISKEY

BLANCO TEQUILA

PISCO

AQUAVIT

MODIFIERS

CYNAR

MARASCHINO LIQUEUR

APEROL

GREEN CHARTREUSE

AROMATIC BITTERS

BIANCO VERMOUTH

FINO SHERRY

OXIDATIVE SHERRY: AMONTILLADO, OLOROSO, OR PALO CORTADO

Now you can also make these classics:

ADONIS

BAMBOO

BENSONHURST

BIJOU

BOULEVARDIER

FANCY FREE

MANHATTAN

MARTINEZ

OLD-FASHIONED

LAST WORD

SIESTA

KNOW THE CLASSICS

Christine Wiseman with her punchy, herbal drink, The Banger (page 114)

LIQUID VACATION

DAIQUIRIS, SWIZZLES, AND BEACHY BLENDER DRINKS

If we get right down to it, all cocktails are a form of escapism. But the ones in this chapter turn the volume on that vibe all the way up. They're the "wish you were here" postcards of cocktails, manifesting white sand, blue seas, and palm trees. We drink these to go to a place that asks no more of us than to ease back, soak up the sun.

Calling for a drink that's "fun," "tropical," or "fruity" is a desperate cry for a vacation in a glass. There are many ways to transport through the classics, be it by way of a lighter, sunshiney citrus drink, such as a daiquiri or margarita, or something in the juicy, spiced, gin-based realm like a Saturn (page 256), or a rich cocktail that's layered with rums, like a coconutty Painkiller. It's just a matter of deciding where you dream of laying out your beach towel—Sayulita? Montego Bay? Copacabana?

Most of these classic tropical drinks we're describing here draw straight from the tiki canon. Much has been written and discussed about tiki style and the cultural appropriation that came with it. We have no interest in perpetuating that, but it is worth giving some historical context to the cocktails themselves. In the mid 1930s, post-Prohibition, Don the Beachcomber and Trader Vic opened bars in California, each finding fame by combining rums and whimsical syrups in secret concoctions, defining the makings of a tiki cocktail. By the 1950s, many Americans were seeking post-war reprieve and the category exploded through the seventies. Over the last fifteen years, we've seen another massive resurgence of cocktails made in this vein.

There's such a spectrum with these drinks, from the unassuming daiquiri (page 256), a rum sour that's beloved by bartenders for the prowess required to perfect the drink; to the Queen's Park Swizzle (page 257), a cocktail that relies on mint, lime, and rum, but finds its groove when swizzled (see page 126) in a tall glass over crushed ice until the glass is covered in a thin coating of ice; to a Zombie, which is a field day of rums and syrups. Often, the uniting theme of tiki and tropical drinks is that they are extremely extra: Extra booze! Extra syrups! So many juices! And, oh, the garnishes! The name of the game is layering spirits and other ingredients and building flavor through multiple components.

A New Take on Tropical

——●-•

Today's best bartenders are proving that these drinks can expand in many directions beyond rum and coconut cream, finding, perhaps, a little more balance with sour and bitter flavors, while still giving them room to be their extravagant selves.

We welcome these modifications not only because it makes our palate much larger, but odds are, we don't all have twelve different rums on our home bar. There's plenty of room in these drinks to swap in other spirits like whiskey or mezcal (see

Ivy's take on a mai tai, the Tia Mia on page 123), or even split the base of a drink to gain complexity, so that it's no longer just rums mingling with one another. Sometimes more is MORE and more is good. Take the Suffering Bastard (page 255), for example. A classic drink that combines cognac and gin (who knew?!) with mint and ginger beer—interesting and tropical in the best botanical way. It's one of our favorite classics in the Speed Rack spec book, along with the unusual Barbary Coast (page 257) that marries gin and scotch.

Maybe you have a bourbon that's on the sweeter side, with coconut and caramel flavors from its time spent aging in a barrel, that could stand in for or be split with rum. Lynnette's Smoke Show (page 134) puts smoky Islay scotch in a piña colada variation. Detecting these flavor similarities gives you so much to play around with in a tropical drink. Or swap in amontillado or oloroso sherry to lower the ABV. Both are barrel aged and deliciously oxidative, which can bring in the nutty, almond notes or baking spices, like cinnamon, that traditionally have a strong presence in classic tiki drinks.

For so long, we've seen the balance of this style of drink hang in the interplay of sweet and sour, but more and more bitter ingredients are finding a place, playing off sweeter tropical juices. There's one classic in the genre that stands out for playing the bitter card: the Jungle Bird (page 256). It's a cocktail that dates to 1978 in Kuala Lumpur, but it has mounted a huge comeback in recent years as amaro has become more popular. The drink combines dark, rich blackstrap rum with Campari, pineapple, and lime. Now modern bartenders are finding inroads into other classics, employing Montenegro, Fernet, and other amari. See page 139 for Claudia Cabrera Rodriguez's Branca Colada, swapping out rum entirely for cooling Fernet Menta. And while the thought of

Carthusian monks is about as anti-vacation vibe as you can get, adding something as random as Chartreuse to a daiquiri will give it an unexpected but awesome herbal complexity. Keep it French and add some rhum agricole from Martinique for a vacation *à la plage*.

The Lime and the Coconut

If you're going the route of a drink that's tropical and fruity, be it pineapple, guava, mango, or passion fruit, odds are you'll need some extra acid for balance, be it classic lemon or lime, or verjus (made from unripe wine grapes), or a techier blend of citric and ascorbic acid for tang without extra flavor.

Fresh fruit is great, but there's so much variation from one mango, say, to the next. Working with purees or shrubs is a more consistent way to bring in fruit flavor. And then there are the many liqueurs, in every fruit flavor imaginable, that in small amounts will give a cocktail fruitiness without going overboard. Even oft-maligned banana-flavored liqueurs are getting love these days; when used gently, they can add intrigue and complexity. For evidence, see Sian Buchan's variation on an old-fashioned, La Isla Bonita (page 119).

Aside from warm-weather fruit juices and purees, don't ignore spice-route flavors like cinnamon, nutmeg, and allspice that are found along the equator. If you're into tropical vibe drinks, buying a bottle of velvet falernum for punches and a little of allspice dram for Navy grog-style drinks is a good idea. You can use these in small amounts for maximum effect. But we also recommend digging around in your kitchen pantry. A cinnamon simple syrup or grated nutmeg can bring a lot of depth without having to buy extra bottles.

There is an element of liquid guilty pleasure to these cocktails, especially when a richer ingredient, like coconut cream or orgeat (sweet, creamy almond syrup) is added to the mix. Coco Lopez is the old standby, but it's incredibly sweet. (Some bars have begun to make their own coconut creams or coconut milks for something less processed and for more control over sugar content.) Considering how many alternative milks are out there now, it's a great moment to tinker with coconut milk, or other nut milks (macadamia! pistachio!), and oat milk in this realm, too. And there's a whole little world of boutique orgeat producers that have popped up, as well. Traditionally made from almonds, these upstarts, like Orgeat Works, are broadening the category with other nut varieties. We've also seen bartenders DIY their own for a more authentic flavor and a creamier texture, with some even using avocado pits to avoid allergens. To try your own hand at a very simple orgeat, whip up one of Evelyn Chick's Poolside Barbie cocktails (page 116).

Crushing It

Finally, what would a tiki drink be without its bountiful crushed ice?! In order to achieve tall, cold, frosty transportive cocktails, you're going to need a lot of crushed ice. You probably don't have a fancy pellet ice machine in your basement like a cocktail bar does (maybe you do!). We advise hitting up your local 7-Eleven for party ice. Or break out your canvas Lewis bag or even just a kitchen towel and whack some cubes with a mallet to get that crush.

And then simply find a long straw and your beach blanket and settle in on the living room floor. May all of your worries be washed away with one of these dreamy tropical cocktails.

DEALER'S CHOICE

Give us your best
garden variety,
tropical-yet-
herbaceous cocktail.
Up, please.

CREATOR

CHRISTINE WISEMAN
*Speed Rack competitor,
regional winner,
and judge*

1 ounce (30 ml) Grey Goose White Peach & Rosemary vodka

½ ounce (15 ml) mezcal, preferably Del Maguey Vida

¼ ounce (7.5 ml) St-Germain elderflower liqueur

½ ounce (15 ml) kiwi puree (see Notes)

½ ounce (15 ml) cucumber juice (see Notes)

½ ounce (15 ml) Herb Blend Cordial (recipe follows)

¾ ounce (22.5 ml) lime juice

Marigold, pansy, or other edible flower, for garnish

THE BANGER

Christine Wiseman is the human manifestation of vacation-in-a-glass. Her sunglasses are big, her smile is bright and twinkly, and if she's not on the beach, she should be. Christine originally devised this drink (photo on page 110) to be served poolside at Broken Shaker, a scene-y bar that sits atop the roof of the Freehand Hotel in Los Angeles. "It's everything I love in one cocktail," she says. There are so many layers to this freewheeling drink: fruitiness from a peach-kissed vodka, light smoke and tropical notes from the agave, cooling cucumber juice and kiwi puree, and a fresh-from-the-garden cordial that she makes using whatever herbs she has on hand. Christine's preferred herb trio is mint, sage, and rosemary—a "fresh, robust, and round combo," she says. The resulting jade-green cocktail is essentially an escape hatch. Christine recommends double straining this cocktail to extract any pulp and sneaky kiwi seeds for a nicely silky drink.

HOW TO MAKE THE DRINK

Add all the ingredients to a cocktail shaker filled with ice. Shake until cold and double strain into a chilled coupe. Garnish with the flower and serve.

NOTE For the kiwi puree, Christine says you can either buy frozen (see Resources, page 259) or peel 4 kiwis and blend them with a little bit of water in a blender until smooth. For the cucumber juice, either put one small, whole cucumber (skin on) through a juicer or blend and strain through a fine-mesh strainer to remove solids.

Herb Blend Cordial

Makes about 1½ cups (360 ml)

¼ cup (about 15 g) fresh herbs (choose 3 kinds)

1 cup (200 g) granulated sugar

Prepare an ice bath. Bring a pot of water to boil. Rinse the herbs. When the water is simmering, submerge the herbs for 10 seconds. Remove them from the water and immediately dunk them in the ice bath. Add the sugar, 1 cup (240 ml) water, and the herbs to a blender and blend until fully integrated. Strain through a fine-mesh strainer into an airtight container and store in the refrigerator for up to 1 week.

THE SPEED RACK GUIDE TO
BUILDING A DRINK

Here's the proper order in which to build individual drinks efficiently and cost effectively, beginning with the least expensive ingredients to avoid any pricey mistakes:

1. Bitters. Adding them first is the best way to not forget them.

2. Citrus. We cannot stress enough the importance of tasting citrus before using it in drinks—it varies widely and will affect the next step.

3. Sugar/syrups. The balance between sweet and tart in a cocktail is essential to the flavor profile of the drink. Adjust as necessary.

4. Mint, cream, fruit, botanicals, egg whites.

5. Muddle. Remember! Muddling is done to release essential oils in herbs or fruits being used in a cocktail. It should be done firmly and with intent.

6. Modifiers. Ingredients such as liqueurs, amari, fortified wines, etc. can be added at this time.

7. Spirits. Liquor is added last, and only to a drink that has been properly measured and balanced.

ABOVE: Christina Chae seeks redemption in Season 10 in New Orleans.

DEALER'S
CHOICE

—

I like tropical gin-
based cocktails.
Can you give me
something tall with
crushed ice?

POOLSIDE BARBIE

Evelyn Chick was one of the first Canadians to cross the border to compete in Speed Rack Seattle and was a member of the inaugural Speed Rack Canada competition in Vancouver the next year. Once we snagged her, we didn't let her go, and she became our local coordinator for years after. "Speed Rack gave me the confidence to mentor others in the same realm and from that solidify other talents that I didn't know I have as a leader," Evelyn says. Today, her expertise is accessible to everyone via online classes and workshops that she runs through her own company, EC Projects. For this Dealer's Choice for the Speed Rack book, Evelyn lucked out—gin is her favorite spirit to mix with. "When I think 'poolside' I think overtly sweet cocktails, umbrellas everywhere, but this is sophisticated in a way where it's still playful, fun, and full of color," she says. Loosely inspired by a mai tai (page 256), this cocktail matches dark, fruity sloe gin with nutty amontillado sherry and a homemade orgeat that Evelyn blends up using cashew milk—rather than the more traditional almond—and rose water for more complexity. "Use it to add texture and creaminess to your cocktails so you can skip the dairy," she says. She recommends saving a little for your coffee the next morning, too. Don't mind if we do!

CREATOR

EVELYN CHICK
*Speed Rack competitor
and coordinator*

---

1 ounce (30 ml) sloe gin

1 ounce (30 ml) amontillado sherry

½ ounce (15 ml) Cashew Orgeat (recipe follows)

¾ ounce (22.5 ml) lime juice

3 drops Angostura or other aromatic bitters

Mint sprig and dehydrated or fresh lime wheel for garnish

HOW TO MAKE THE DRINK

Add all the ingredients to a cocktail shaker and shake vigorously for 10 to 15 seconds. Strain into a rocks glass filled with fresh ice. Garnish with a mint sprig and lime wheel, and serve.

Cashew Orgeat

Makes about 1½ cups (360 ml)

1 cup (240 ml) unsweetened cashew milk

2 cups (400 g) granulated sugar

1 teaspoon rose water

In a blender, combine the cashew milk and sugar. Blend on medium-low speed for 2 to 3 minutes. Then slowly turn it up to medium speed and blend for another 2 to 3 minutes. Blend until there are no more visible sugar granules. Add the rose water. Pulse the blender a few times to integrate.

Bottle and refrigerate for up to 3 weeks. This can also be used to glam up your mai tais (page 256).

We'd like a nightcap
you'd have on a
holiday—an old-
fashioned variation
please! Any aged
spirit with tropical
flavors will do!

LA ISLA BONITA

The old-fashioned template (spirit, sugar, bitters) has been endlessly riffed upon—understandable for a drink that's been around since the early 1800s. Most people will know it in its original form, with a base of bourbon or rye whiskey, but to make it beach-appropriate, Sian Buchan started with an aged agave spirit, reposado tequila, which has a subtle oakiness of its own. Here the reposado's spice—think tropical cinnamon and nutmeg—meets up with a ripe banana liqueur and coconut syrup, with an absinthe rinse standing in for bitters. (To rinse a glass, swirl a little bit of absinthe around the interior of the glass to coat it and then discard any excess.) "You want to dilute the drink by about 25 percent as it will dilute a bit more over the ice you serve it in," says Sian. "So, if it tastes a bit strong when you first try it, leave it to dilute a touch more before you enjoy it." It should come around pretty quickly, if served on a warm evening. Best served with a musical pairing from the Queen of Pop, Madonna, like the cocktail's name, "La Isla Bonita," suggests.

CREATOR

SIAN BUCHAN
Speed Rack competitor

Absinthe, for rinsing

1½ ounces (45 ml) reposado
tequila, preferably Tequila
Ocho

½ ounce (15 ml) banana
liqueur, preferably Giffard
Banane du Brésil

¼ ounce (7.5 ml) coconut
syrup (see Resources,
page 259)

HOW TO MAKE THE DRINK

Rinse a rocks glass with absinthe. Add the rest of the ingredients to a mixing glass filled with ice. Stir until cold and strain into the prepared glass over a large ice cube. Serve.

DEALER'S CHOICE

Give us a daiquiri riff but with coastal vibes that represent your roots—Lima meets Charleston.

CREATOR

FABIANA PINILLOS
Speed Rack competitor, regional winner

1½ ounces (45 ml) white rum, preferably Probitas Blended

½ ounce (15 ml) velvet falernum

1 ounce (30 ml) Chicha Morada Syrup (recipe follows)

¾ ounce (22.5 ml) lime juice

Cinnamon stick and a straw (optional), for garnish

CHIQUITA LINDA

"I never thought a competition could change so much in someone," says Fabiana Pinillos, who won in the Southeast competition in Charleston, South Carolina, in Season 11. "Speed Rack gives you roots to such amazing humans—ties you to a family that will grow with you, and an unimaginable number of people wanting the best things for you." We are grateful to have Fabiana's unbridled joy and enthusiasm for all things pink in our Speed Rack family. For this Dealer's Choice, a classic daiquiri (page 256) is bolstered with tropical Velvet Falernum and given a purple flair. Its hue comes via a warming spice–infused syrup inspired by chicha morada, her favorite drink in her native Peru, which is made from dried purple corn and is extremely flavorful and refreshing. In Peru, every household has its own take on chicha morada. This recipe makes a lot of syrup, and you will have leftovers, but it is an amazing ingredient to play with in other spirituous (pisco sours!) or no-proof cocktails, or simply serve on ice. Rather than serving it up, as is traditional with daiquiris, Fabiana pours this over crushed ice in a Collins glass for maximum chill. A happy meeting indeed.

HOW TO MAKE THE DRINK

Combine all the ingredients in a shaker filled with ice. Shake until chilled and strain into a Collins glass. Fill the glass with crushed ice over the top. Grate the cinnamon over the top of the drink, and, if you have one, stick a straw in for easy drinking. Serve.

Chicha Morada Syrup

Makes 4 cups (960 ml)

⅔ cup (110 g) dried purple corn (see Resources, page 259)

Skin and core of 1 small pineapple (6 to 8 ounces/ 170 to 225 grams)

2 cinnamon sticks

½ teaspoon freshly grated nutmeg

10 whole cloves

3½ cups (680 g) sugar

Combine all the ingredients with 3 cups (720 ml) water in a medium pot and place over medium heat. Simmer for 15 minutes, then remove from the heat. Strain out the solids into another heat-safe container with a lid, and let cool. This syrup will keep in the refrigerator for 4 weeks.

Make this for
someone who likes
the smoky, funky side
of tropical.

TIA MIA

CREATOR

IVY MIX
Speed Rack co-founder

1 ounce (30 ml) mezcal, preferably Del Maguey Vida

1 ounce (30 ml) Jamaican rum, preferably Appleton Signature

½ ounce (15 ml) orange Curaçao, preferably Pierre Ferrand

½ ounce (15 ml) orgeat, preferably Orgeat Works Toasted Almond Orgeat (see Resources, page 259)

¾ ounce (22.5 ml) lime juice

An orchid (food-safe, please), mint sprig, and lime wheel, for garnish

I made this drink when I was working for Julie Reiner at her now-closed Lani Kai. We had a delicious mai tai (page 256) on the menu there and I started experimenting with adding a little mezcal float . . . because who doesn't love that? Eventually, I outright split the base of my mai tais with mezcal, giving added dimension to a drink that can often feel like a pileup of rums. Even with the layers of Jamaican rum funk and mezcal smoke, the drink remains breezy and refreshing, which is in large part thanks to the toasted almond orgeat that I love from Orgeat Works, which has more of a roasted quality than your classic marzipan-y white kind. Any orgeat will make a delicious drink here, but if you can find this one, all the better. Don't forget to dress the drink with an orchid for swift transport to the waves of Oaxaca.

HOW TO MAKE THE DRINK

Add all the ingredients to a cocktail shaker filled with ice and shake until cold. Strain into a large rocks glass over crushed ice and garnish with the orchid, mint sprig, and lime wheel. Serve.

DEALER'S CHOICE

Blend us up! What kind of blended tropical goodness can you make us? Put us at the beach!

CREATOR

YAEL STORMBORN
Speed Rack competitor, USA national winner

Lime Leaf Salt (recipe follows), for rim

1½ ounces (45 ml) Ketel One Botanical Mint & Cucumber vodka

¾ ounce (22.5 ml) lime juice

½ ounce (15 ml) Suze gentian aperitif

½ ounce (15 ml) St-Germain elderflower liqueur

½ ounce (15 g) granulated sugar

1 tablespoon Cane Sugar Mix (page 260)

Big pinch salt

1½ ounces (45 ml) sour gose beer, preferably Wiseacre The Beach Within Reach or Dogfish Head SeaQuench Ale

Bouquet of fresh mint leaves and 2 cucumber wheels, for garnish

FROZEN IGUANA

When we first launched Speed Rack, Yael Stormborn was working with Lynnette at Peels in New York City, which meant that she essentially had no choice but to compete in the first-ever Speed Rack. "Naturally, I wouldn't dream of saying no to Lynnette," she jokes, "but I also love a good challenge." She left the champion not only of the first ever New York City event, but also of the entire first season! Yael's led beverage programs around the world and today she runs her own creative events production company, which calls on her talents as a dancer and performer, as well as behind the bar. When Yael took the stage in Speed Rack, Dealer's Choice wasn't yet a part of the competition, but she fully understood the assignment here. The "beer-ito" (that is, a frozen mojito topped with beer) was a family of drinks she concocted while working in Nashville at a rooftop bar. With doses of Suze and St-Germain, this iteration is floral, herbal, and salty—thanks both to a big pinch of salt and a glug of sour gose-style beer added just before serving. A bit of sea spray, if you will.

HOW TO MAKE THE DRINK

Rim half of a hurricane glass with the lime leaf salt. Add all the ingredients, except the sour beer, to a blender pitcher. Add 1 cup (240 ml) crushed ice and blend until smooth. Add the sour beer and give the pitcher a quick swirl. Pour into the prepared hurricane glass. Garnish with the bouquet of mint and place the cucumber wheels in the glass. Serve.

Lime Leaf Salt   *Makes 5 tablespoons (55 g)*

3 tablespoons (45 g) coarse kosher salt

1 tablespoon lime leaf powder (see Resources, page 259)

1 tablespoon curry powder

Combine all the ingredients in a small airtight nonreactive container and stir to mix well. Store in a dry place indefinitely.

DEALER'S CHOICE

Hello, Texas! Give us that Texas tiki goodness. Crushed ice and two base spirits, please.

CREATOR

SARAH TROXELL
Speed Rack competitor, regional and USA national winner

6 to 8 fresh mint leaves

1 ounce (30 ml) mezcal, preferably Del Maguey Vida

½ ounce (15 ml) white rum, preferably Wray & Nephew Overproof

½ ounce (15 ml) green Chartreuse

½ ounce (15 ml) Chinola passion fruit liqueur

1 ounce (30 ml) lime juice

½ ounce (15 ml) Rich Simple Syrup (page 261)

1 dash Saline Solution (page 262, see note)

6 dashes Peychaud's bitters

Bouquet of fresh mint and a lime wedge, for garnish

SWIZZLED IN SISTERHOOD

There's something sort of contagious about the energy that surrounds Speed Rack. So many of our competitors attend events or witness a colleague training and are compelled to sign up, too. Such is the case with Sarah Troxell, who watched Elyse Blechman practicing rounds and thought, "It's a sport I might actually be good at for once." And good she was! Sarah was our national winner in Season 4. Her go-to classic is the Queen's Park Swizzle (page 257) and it was a reference for this drink. "Tropical beach drinks are my favorite style to create. They allow my culinary experience to shine by balancing bold flavors and spirits." This is bold in every direction from the mezcal and overproof rum split base to vibrant passion fruit liqueur and a helping of green Chartreuse that will certainly make the drinker wonder, "What *is* that?!" While a swizzle stick (harvested from a tree native to certain Caribbean islands) is surely a cool thing to have, Sarah says it won't make or break the drink; swizzling with a long barspoon or even a knife will do the trick. The goal is to agitate the drink, almost like a whisk would, so as to aerate and dilute it. Consider the swizzle stick a Caribbean pre-blender blender. Just make sure to get the glass frosty cold.

HOW TO MAKE THE DRINK

Place the mint leaves in the bottom of a Collins glass and add all the ingredients, except the bitters. Fill the glass two-thirds of the way with crushed ice. Swizzle the drink using a swizzle stick or a long spoon until the ingredients are well chilled and incorporated. Fill the glass (and then some) with crushed ice and top with the Peychaud's bitters. Garnish with the mint bouquet and lime wedge, and serve.

CREATOR

IVY MIX
Speed Rack co-founder

1½ ounces (45 ml) oloroso sherry, preferably Lustau

¾ ounce (22.5 ml) Plantation Stiggins' Fancy Pineapple rum

¾ ounce (22.5 ml) lime juice

½ ounce (15 ml) Cane Syrup (page 260)

Lime wheel, for garnish

DAY RAY OFF

Ah, the daiquiri, the most famous of rum sours and darling of bartenders everywhere. Many adhere to the classic template of 2 parts rum to ¾ part sugar and ¾ part lime, but this cocktail has been incrementally tinkered with by bartenders looking to perfect the ratios for years. For a drink with only three ingredients, there are so many variables: What rum are you using? What sweetener are you using? How tart is the juice from the specific lime you're using? There's plenty of space for reinventing and rethinking here. The beauty and danger of the drink is that it's delightfully easy to knock back, which is why I devised this lower-alc version that's based in oloroso sherry with just a touch of pineapple rum, which gives roundness and a little kick. Should you only have simple syrup on hand, just swap in ¾ ounce (22.5 ml) for the cane syrup. And then proceed drinking, preferably in a sunlit locale all afternoon.

HOW TO MAKE THE DRINK

Add all the ingredients to a cocktail shaker filled with ice. Shake until cold and strain into a chilled cocktail glass. Express the lime wheel over the drink and place it on the edge of the glass; serve.

CREATOR

ERIN HAYES
Speed Rack competitor

---

2 ounces (60 ml) Pandan-Infused Aged White Rum (recipe follows)

¾ ounce (22.5 ml) lime juice

¾ ounce (22.5 ml) Cinnamon Syrup (page 260)

3 ounces (90 ml) unsweetened grapefruit-flavored sparkling water, preferably LaCroix Pamplemousse

1 dash absinthe

Grapefruit twist, for garnish

ROCKET QUEEN

A Speed Rack queen we first met in Chicago, Erin Hayes moved on to become a huge part of the current LA cocktail scene. Goth glam through and through, she also runs the Black Lagoon, a Halloween cocktail pop-up series that tours the country, with Speed Rack Canada and UK alum Kelsey Ramage. Strange though it may seem, Erin's Chicago roots play a big role in her love of the escapism of this cocktail genre. She worked at Chicago's tropical-focused Lost Lake before moving to LA, the birthplace of the canon. "Tropical drinks will forever hold a special place in my heart, but these days I'm all about utilizing unexpected flavor combinations," says Erin. This is her lightened-up, more refreshing version of a tropical drink, in the form of a Collins. Hayes says she always gravitates toward rum for its versatility and complexity and here she starts with an aged white rum (her preference is El Dorado 3 Year), which brings a "round, rich element of flavor" that's furthered when infused with sweet, grassy, almost vanilla-scented leaves from the tropical pandan plant. She pairs this with one of her go-to flavor pairings, grapefruit and cinnamon, in a tall, bubbly, multilayered drink. The infused rum also makes a nice addition to mojitos and daiquiris. And if you're too lazy to make it yourself, this cocktail can be found in cans nationwide as part of Erin's LiveWire Drinks collection.

HOW TO MAKE THE DRINK

Add all the ingredients to a Collins glass filled with ice. Stir gently to incorporate. Express the grapefruit twist over the drink and discard. Serve.

Pandan-Infused Aged White Rum
Makes 2 cups (480 ml)

2 cups (480 ml) aged white rum (such as El Dorado 3 Year or Bounty White)

5 frozen pandan leaves (50 g) (see Resources, page 259)

Combine the rum and pandan in an airtight container and let infuse for 4 hours. Strain through a fine-mesh strainer and store at room temperature for up to 1 month.

CREATOR

KATIE STIPE
friend of Speed Rack

1½ ounces (45 ml) blanco
tequila, preferably Olmeca
Altos Plata

¾ ounce (22.5 ml) lime juice

¾ ounce (22.5 ml) Simple
Syrup (page 262)

½ ounce (15 ml) grapefruit
juice

¼ ounce (7.5 ml) Campari

Lime wheel, for garnish

SIESTA

Katie Stipe has been with us since the beginning. She was one of the first women to work *behind* the bar in envelope-pushing New York City cocktail bars in the early 2000s. She currently lives and works in Portland, Oregon, where she's helped us organize Speed Rack events. Katie created this drink back in 2006 when she and Lynnette were working together at New York's Flatiron Lounge, owned by Speed Rack mentor and queen Julie Reiner. It's a riff on the classic Hemingway Daiquiri (page 256), and for whatever mystical mixological reason, it caught on and stuck—this drink is now served in cocktail bars around the world. Katie's variation swaps the usual white rum with blanco tequila and the maraschino with Campari, for a take that is bolder in every way—grassy, bitter, just a touch sweet—while remaining balanced. "At the time the Siesta was developed, our cocktail Rolodex was greatly lacking in solid agave-based recipes," says Katie. "Tequila and mezcal really took off in the years to follow." For others, it was a gateway to drinks with a more bitter edge—well before the Negroni boom. All classic drinks see an evolution over time—endless riffs—and Katie admits that even she has tinkered with the specs for the Siesta over the years, to cater to her guests as necessary. "Sometimes I have bumped the tequila up to 1¾ ounces or 2 ounces. And I tend to go heavier on the lime juice and do a scant pour of simple syrup, plus a wee pinch of salt doesn't hurt either," she says.

HOW TO MAKE THE DRINK

Add all the ingredients in a shaker filled with ice. Shake until cold and strain into a chilled coupe or cocktail glass. Garnish with the lime wheel, and serve.

FROM THE FOUNDERS

Make this for whiskey-loving friends who want a creamy drink.

CREATOR

LYNNETTE
MARRERO
Speed Rack co-founder

½ ounce (22.5 ml)
Demerara Syrup (page 260)

¾ ounce (22.5 ml) coconut
cream

1 ounce (30 ml) oloroso
sherry, preferably Lustau

1 ounce (30 ml) Laphroaig
or other smoky scotch, such
as Caol Ila

1 whole egg

Freshly grated nutmeg, for
garnish

SMOKE SHOW

For this, I call on my Puerto Rican roots. Christmastime in Puerto Rico is all about coquito, a coconut milk–based drink (in a similar vein as eggnog) for which every family has its own signature recipe. This one is based on the formula for a classic "flip"-style drink, which involves vigorously shaking a spirit with sugar and a whole egg, resulting in something rich and creamy. Coquito is traditionally made with rum, but this is based in Laphroaig, a bold and peaty scotch from Islay. Scotch and coconut are one of those magical combinations that seems completely out of place, like a kilt on a beach, but it works. I rein in the ABV by splitting the base with oloroso sherry, which is lower in proof. Want to make this cocktail vegan? Substitute the whole egg for an ounce (30 ml) aquafaba (the liquid from a can of chickpeas) and increase the coconut cream to 1 ounce (30 ml).

HOW TO MAKE THE DRINK

Add the syrup, coconut cream, sherry, and scotch to one tin of a cocktail shaker. Crack the egg into the other tin, making sure no shells get inside. Assemble the two tins and dry shake (no ice) until the ingredients are combined. Open the shaker, add ice, and shake until cold. Strain into a coupe, garnish with nutmeg, and serve.

FROM LEFT TO RIGHT:
Not a Piña Colada (page 137),
Pineapple Crown (page 139),
Branca Colada (page 139)

SPEED RACK
· SPINS ·
THE
· CLASSICS ·

Piña Colada

The epitome of a vacation drink, the piña colada has found its way from swim-up bars to frozen cocktail machines on the Coney Island boardwalk to fancy coupes at the world's top bars. Here, three Speed Rack iterations that stretch to the far corners of the drink's identity.

PIÑA COLADA

2 ounces (60 ml) rum, light or aged

½ ounce (15 ml) lime juice

1 ounce (30 ml) pineapple juice

1 ounce (30 ml) cream of coconut

1 ounce (30 ml) coconut milk

Pineapple wedge and a cocktail umbrella, for garnish

Add all the ingredients to a blender with 2 cups (480 ml) ice. Blend on high until smooth. Pour into a Collins or hurricane glass. Garnish with the pineapple wedge and cocktail umbrella and serve.

Not a Piña Colada

CREATOR

KAREN TARTT, *Speed Rack competitor*

Karen Tartt's path as a bartender has taken all sorts of detours, but just after competing in Season 8, she was sidelined with a type of chronic migraine. "I received messages and calls from the women I had just trained and competed with encouraging me to not give up. I can't begin to tell you how much those meant to me and kept me going during early recovery," she says of the fellow women+ she met through Speed Rack. She has since launched a consulting business that creates cocktails for people with migraines and inflammatory disorders. A piña colada could be a landmine drink for those with inflammation: "Pineapple is a common trigger for those sensitive to citrus. Most coconut creams contain gums or other additives that can be problematic. Unaged spirits are best for folks with sensitivity issues," she says. Here, Karen has entirely rethought what the drink can be. To get the right fruitiness and tanginess of a piña colada, she uses a blend of peaches and apples with ascorbic and citric acids (see Resources, page 259), coconut cream finds a toasty edge—and white rum is infused with dandelion root, rooibos tea, and vanilla for the depth, fullness, and caramelly side of a barrel-aged rum. This is the ultimate Dealer's Choice expression, but definitely requires time, which is to say: Plan ahead for the pool party and you will not be disappointed.

2 ounces (60 ml) Not Pineapple (recipe follows)

2 ounces (60 ml) Seedy Coconut Cream (recipe follows)

1½ ounces (45 ml) Dandelion Root–Rooibos Rum (recipe follows)

Colorful edible flower, for garnish

Add all the ingredients to a shaker tin. Add crushed ice and give the drink a few quick shakes before pouring it into a Collins glass or tropical mug—including the ice. Add more crushed ice to fill the glass, garnish with the flower, and serve.

(recipe continued)

NOT PINEAPPLE

Makes 16 ounces (480 ml)

1 pound (455 g) ripe yellow peaches

2 pounds (910 g) Granny Smith apples

1 teaspoon (6 g) ascorbic acid

1 teaspoon (6 g) citric acid

Slice the peaches into cubes that are manageable for your juicer, leaving the skins on and discarding the pits. Juice the peaches and let the juice rest for a moment while any foam rises to the top. Strain the juice through a damp cheesecloth, discarding the pulp and foam, and set aside. Cut the apples into pieces that are manageable for your juicer, leaving the skins on and discarding the cores. Add the ascorbic acid to the juice-catching vessel. Juice the apples and let the juice rest for a moment while any foam rises to the top. Strain the juice using a damp cheesecloth, discarding the pulp and foam. Combine the apple and peach juices in a nonreactive glass container and add the citric acid. Seal the container and gently roll back and forth until the citric acid is dissolved. Store in the refrigerator for up to 3 days.

SEEDY COCONUT CREAM

Makes 18 ounces (540 ml)

2 tablespoons (20 g) hemp seeds

⅓ cup (45 g) pumpkin seeds, hulled

½ cup (120 ml) warm water

1 cup (200 g) granulated sugar

¼ teaspoon orange flower water

1 (13.5-ounce / 405 ml) can simple coconut milk, without gums added

In a pan over medium heat, toast the hemp seeds. Add to a blender pitcher when fragrant. Repeat the process with the pumpkin seeds until you hear a slight crackling. Add the pumpkin seeds and the warm water to the blender. Blend on medium speed for about 15 seconds. Repeat if the seeds are not fully broken up. Pour the nut mixture into a medium saucepan and add the coconut milk, sugar, and orange flower water. Cook over medium heat, stirring until the sugar is fully dissolved. Remove from the heat and cool to room temperature. Strain through cheesecloth into an airtight container and store in the refrigerator for up to 1 week.

DANDELION ROOT-ROOIBOS RUM

Makes 16 ounces (480 ml)

½ vanilla bean

1½ teaspoons (3 g) dried rooibos tea

2 tablespoons (18 g) roasted, dried dandelion root tea (see Resources, page 259)

16 ounces (480 ml) white, unaged rhum agricole, preferably Rhum Clément Blanc

Split the vanilla bean lengthwise and scrape the seeds into a lidded glass jar. Add the vanilla bean pod, rooibos tea, dandelion root tea, and rum, and gently roll back and forth. Let the rum infuse at room temperature for 24 hours, occasionally agitating it. Strain the rum through a fine-mesh sieve and pour back into the jar. It will keep at room temperature for up to 2 months.

Branca Colada

CREATOR
CLAUDIA CABRERA RODRIGUEZ
Speed Rack competitor and judge

"I just love piña coladas, but sometimes they're a bit too sweet and overpowering," says Claudia Cabrera Rodriguez, who competed in our first Speed Rack competition in Mexico City in 2019. Fernet Branca Menta, a bitter Italian amaro made with a hefty dose of peppermint, tends to be used sparingly in drinks because it can overwhelm other flavors, but here Claudia uses it brilliantly as the base for her piña colada—omitting rum altogether. The bitterness of the amaro balances out the sweetness of the rest of the drink. "This makes it more fresh and, well, to be honest you could pound a few." Her recipe is meant to be made in a blender, but Claudia says that it does just fine when shaken well and served in a tall glass over crushed ice.

2 ounces (60 ml) Fernet Branca Menta

2 ounces (60 ml) pineapple juice

½ ounce (15 ml) lime juice

½ ounce (15 ml) Simple Syrup (page 262)

1 ounce (30 ml) coconut cream

3 dashes Angostura bitters

Lime wheels and pineapple leaves, for garnish

Add all the ingredients, except the bitters, to a blender with 1 cup (240 ml) ice. Blend until smooth. Pour into a highball glass, add the dashes of bitters, and garnish with the lime wheels and pineapple leaves. Serve.

Pineapple Crown

CREATOR
LYNNETTE MARRERO
Speed Rack co-founder

I might not love rich and creamy dessert drinks, but I do love a piña colada . . . a small one. I built this variation to be lighter in alcohol (it has a split-base of two sherries) and lighter overall, with a 50/50 blend of coconut cream and cashew milk (for those with nut allergies, sub oat milk or soy milk) and a portion of coconut water. It's my ideal colada—easily batched for a crowd and delicious over crushed ice or blended and served frozen.

1 ounce (30 ml) cream sherry

1 ounce (30 ml) palo cortado sherry

1 ounce (30 ml) pineapple juice

1 ounce (30 ml) coconut cream/cashew milk blend

¾ ounce (22.5 ml) coconut water

½ ounce (15 ml) lime juice

½ ounce (15 ml) Vanilla Syrup (page 262)

Pinch sea salt

1 crack black pepper

Pineapple wedge and fronds and Angostura bitters, for garnish

Add all the ingredients to a cocktail shaker with 2 ice cubes. Whip-shake until cold. Pour into a highball glass, tropical cocktail mug, or large margarita glass. Add crushed ice to fill the glass. Garnish with the pineapple wedge and fronds and 4 to 6 dashes of Angostura bitters. Serve.

For the frozen version: Add all the ingredients to a blender with ¼ cup (60 ml) cracked ice per serving. Blend until smooth and garnish as noted above.

In Season 10, Baylee Hopings was victorious in Speed Rack Southeast with her quick moves and signature style.

THE SPEED RACK GUIDE TO BUILDING A ROUND

There is a method to the madness. Every good bartender will have a blueprint in mind for the steps to build a round of drinks so that when they're served to guests, the highballs are still fizzy, drinks on the rocks aren't watery, and the martinis are still cold. Speed Rack presents its own challenges (namely, very hot lights and bodies rushing around), but the order of operations you follow on a busy Friday night at the service bar applies just as much to making a round at home as it does to when you're onstage in competition. Here's our map for efficiently building a round of drinks:

1. Set up your glassware in the sequence the drinks are ordered, from left to right. If any of the drinks you're making will be served up, put ice in those glasses to get them cooling down. Then set up your necessary shakers and mixing glasses. Be meticulous about organizing your tools (jiggers, weighted shaker tins, mixing glass, and strainers), a speed rail or your bar cart at home, juices, and syrups so that you never have to go searching. You will eventually build the muscle memory to not have to look when you need something. You will simply know where it is, reach for it, and pick it up.

2. Start with your highballs and Collinses—drinks that are built in the glass. Add the ingredients to the glass, leaving the ice and carbonated mixers to be added at the last minute.

3. Then get working on the stirred drinks, such as old-fashioneds, martinis, Manhattans, etc. These drinks require the most attention and will start to deteriorate as soon as they're poured. That said, they do require chilling and dilution from ice. Get this started while you're working on your other drinks.

4. Next come shaken (margaritas, daiquiris, gimlets, etc.), swizzled, more complex built drinks that incorporate sugar and herbs, and blender drinks. These drinks should be constructed, simultaneously and methodically, in shakers or swizzled directly in the serving glass. Ice is added last, and, if possible, into the side of the shaker set opposite the one in which the drink was built. This ensures that, if you become distracted, the ice is not diluting the drink, and, if necessary, the melted ice can be discarded without having to throw out the drink and start over.

5. Add ice and top all one-and-ones and highballs in the round with the appropriate mixer.

6. Shake, strain, and pour all shaken cocktails. We like to shake cocktails that will be served over ice first, as, again, they will naturally have slightly more durability.

7. Top any cocktail requiring sparkling wine or something otherwise fizzy.

8. Stir and pour stirred drinks.

9. Garnish and serve.

DEALER'S CHOICE

Please give me a
sustainable daisy or
daiquiri with some
savory notes.

CREATOR

KELSEY RAMAGE
Speed Rack competitor

1½ ounces (45 ml) blanco
tequila

8 to 10 arugula leaves

½ ounce (15 ml) bianco
vermouth

½ ounce (15 ml) lime juice

¼ ounce (7.5 ml) Honey
Syrup (page 260)

1 dash Saline Solution
(page 262)

2 dashes celery bitters

Edible flower or radish
slice, for garnish (if
desired)

FABLE

Kelsey Ramage is our only Speed Rack alum to have competed in three countries—the United States, Canada, and the UK. Over the last eight years, she's been leading an important, global conversation on sustainability in bartending with her Trash Collective, forcing the industry to take a long hard look at its impact when it comes to waste. For this drink, Kelsey wanted to begin with a spirit that was "agricultural and allows the terroir to show through": tequila was a logical pick. Here's a cocktail for someone whose vision for a "liquid vacation" is less about palm trees and more about some quality time among the rows of a dewy, green garden—a weekend on Martha's Vineyard, if you will. "I wanted to bring out the grassy, white pepper notes in the tequila," she told us. "Radish was too harsh, so arugula seemed the right bet. From there, celery bitters for grassiness and a bit of bianco vermouth to soften it all out."

HOW TO MAKE THE DRINK

Add the tequila to a shaker. Then rip up the arugula leaves and drop them in with the tequila. Allow this mixture to infuse for 2 to 5 minutes and then add the rest of the ingredients. Fill the shaker with ice and shake until chilled. Double strain into a chilled coupe. Garnish with an edible flower or a radish slice and serve.

THE SPEED RACK
COMMUNITY

"Obviously, everyone wants to win, but what's been really cool is even if you don't win, even if you don't make it to the top eight, even if you don't make it to the live competition—you have such an amazing support system behind you; we're all in this together and we're all going through the exact same thing," said Haley Traub, our USA national winner in Season 7. "It's a very different competition in that way because we're actually here to have a good time together and support each other and look out for each other."

Considering the extreme training required to compete in Speed Rack—hundreds of practice rounds, color-coded flash cards, shaking and stirring and pouring and memorizing, repeating the same setup and the same steps, tasting for balance, knowing that an old-fashioned gets an orange twist, but that if you're feeling fancy, a lemon wouldn't hurt either—the truly remarkable love and friendship and support that we see between all of our Speed Rackers catches us off guard every time. This is a testament to the community that has grown organically over the years.

When we started, Speed Rack was a competition for "women," but over the last decade, we've learned a lot and evolved this language to be more representative of our commitment to inclusion. Our mission statement remains the same: to create a platform to empower competitors and to celebrate the diverse talent of the hospitality industry that we love so much.

And while it's been honestly mind-blowing to watch how unwavering this bond is on our home turf

in the United States, we've also had front-row seats in cities and countries where female-identifying bartenders are only just beginning to get the attention and command the respect and the jobs that they so deserve. As we have expanded globally, we have consistently received the same message in each new country: "There just aren't enough women here to compete." But with every stop, we have had plenty. So, you tell us, are there just "not enough women?" We haven't found that to be true.

We're often asked if there are any men involved and yes, there sure are! Historically, men have served as barbacks (that's changing, with Speed Rack alums wanting to stay involved), as well as hosts, cheerleaders, and volunteers throughout the event. And we believe that bartenders who are men play a particularly important role in this, especially in places where women bartenders are just starting to take on larger bar roles. We know these women can do it, but the support of the entire community and the people who have traditionally held these roles is crucial. It requires men who have always had the spotlight to take a step back and sincerely and consciously make room for others, even if it's just joining the crowd and clapping. We have seen this play out in wonderful ways in countries like Mexico, which is seeing a massive and exciting cocktail boom, but which has always had a male-dominated industry. To see these bartenders show up on their nights off communicates an awesome change.

We've watched this across Asia, as well, and have seen Speed Rack competitors break glass ceilings

and take on larger and more visible rolls in their communities, including Summer Lo, our second Speed Rack Asia winner in Hong Kong, in 2019, who holds the role of assistant director of Food and Beverage at the Four Seasons there. Yvonne Chen, who also competed in Asia, is head bartender at the same hotel's Ago bar. "Competing in Speed Rack felt like woman power," Summer said. "After I did it, I was proud to tell everyone, 'Yes, I work in a bar.' And then, as a woman, to become part of leadership felt huge. Now you see a lot of women working in bars and I love being a part of that," she says.

But the community is not only built of the competitors; it encompasses our sponsors, our bartending colleagues that come out in droves in every city, the regional coordinators that pull the events off, the hundreds of volunteers that emerge each season (some of whom even travel with us city to city), our DJs, our barbacks, our hosts. Everyone is rooting for these badass competitors. It's so many hugs.

"My first Speed Rack I remember seeing these superhuman women onstage, blazing through rounds and then supporting each other with hugs and high-fives. I knew that I wanted to learn from these women, grow with these women, and eventually bring others into the fold. I was drawn to the fierceness of the sisterhood and that no matter how competitive we all were, we all had each other's backs."

—MARY PALAC

ABOVE: Fabiola Juarez is cheered into the next round by her fellow competitor Kim Vo in New York in Season 11.

KNOW THE CLASSICS

SPICY MARGARITA
BLOODY MARY

SOME LIKE IT HOT

BEYOND THE SPICY MARGARITA

Capsaicin nation! We see your spicy margarita and we're upping the ante. There are some folks who aren't just looking for a little heat, they're looking for sweat-inducing, mouth-on-fire, flames-shooting-out-of-the-glass type heat in their cocktails. And there are those who are looking for just a tingle of chile. But across the board, bartenders are obliging the need for heat.

The most straightforward way to bring some scorch to a cocktail is to infuse chile peppers directly into a base spirit or into syrups. (Plenty of other flavors, from tea to spices to fruit, can be infused in a similar manner. There are examples of these throughout the book.) Because of the alcohol in spirits, they will take on a stronger infusion more quickly than syrups—and when infusing chiles, it's completely unmitigated heat. Once you've done it there's no going back, which is why we'll often infuse just half a bottle rather than the whole thing. A mistake with a spirit is a more costly one than a mistake with a syrup. For an extra-spicy syrup, rather than allowing the chiles to sit in simple syrup and infuse, try blending your chiles of choice into simple syrup (see page 152). It will be *far* spicier and much more vegetal.

Pick a Pepper

It might go without saying that not all chiles are created equal. But we have such great access to peppers—both fresh and dried—in markets across the United States now, it's worth exploring beyond the ubiquitous jalapeño as an easy way to switch things up. From relatively mild and vegetal poblanos to fruity and extremely spicy habaneros on the fresh side and sweet and smoky Kashmiri peppers to rich and earthy guajillos on the dried, there is a huge range of spice levels and flavors.

Habaneros can be 12 to 100 times hotter than a jalapeño, but they also are floral, sweet, and bursting with flavor. Ancho chiles are ripened and dried poblano chiles with a mild heat and sweet smoky flavor. Chipotles, aka smoked and dried overripe jalapeños, give a more intense smoky heat.

Fresh peppers will be bright, tart, and spicy, whereas dried ones tend to have more of a slow burn—still spicy, but in a baritone way. Dried and fresh peppers have the same level of capsaicin, but dried peppers tend to be more concentrated in spice—which is to say, a little can go a long way. That said, the difference in heat level between fresh and dried chiles does not vary too much when you're infusing them into a liquid. The water in the liquid will help distribute the capsaicin equally.

It should be noted that many chiles, especially when fresh, can be wildly inconsistent—one will be kind of mild; another will burn your face off. This has to do with freshness, the time of year, where they were harvested, and just the fact that there is variance with everything in nature. Jalapeños are particularly difficult in this way. We have found serranos to be much more reliably spicy, but just use them knowing that they can turn up the heat very quickly.

A word of caution! Take care when handling peppers. We'd recommend using gloves when working with the notoriously spicy ones, like habaneros or ghost peppers, but know that even the less fiery ones can sneak up on you. Be sure to wash your hands!

Give It a Kick: Liqueurs, Syrups, and Bitters

Over the past decade, the number of chile-based liqueurs available in liquor stores has grown immensely. Ancho Reyes was an early entry into the market in 2014, and has since added a fresher take on their original chipotle-base recipe with a verde poblano-based version. Giffard (a French company with dozens of wonderfully flavored liqueurs) has gotten in the game with its fragrant Piment d'Espelette liqueur. Xila Licor de Agave, an ancho-laced, mezcal-based liqueur, is also a quality example.

While infused spirits, syrups, and spiced liqueurs add volume to a drink, there's also a big array of spicy bitters and other fiery tinctures made today—from smoky chipotle bitters to extreme-heat habanero bitters like Scrappy's Firewater or Bittermens Hellfire—that can give a drink a substantial amount of heat in a matter of dashes. We'll sometimes even use these to further dial up spice in drinks that are already based in chile-infused spirits. Bottled hot sauce can nicely bring warmth to a drink, too (as in Gigi Temprano's Buffalo Soldier, page 163), but we mostly only use those in Bloody Mary–style drinks or micheladas because they're a little harder to control. Some are sweeter, or some lean into savory flavors, like onion or garlic. And, often, they'll also have a little bit of vinegar in the mix, which can impact the acidity of a drink; and that can be great, but only if that's what you're looking for.

Other ingredients, like pink and black peppercorns, will bring heat in a less puckery, more savory way; they play well in syrups with other culinary flavors, like vanilla or strawberry. Or you can use them to make a kicky tincture as Jess Yurko does in her complex after-dinner drink Talking in Cursive (page 244). Peppercorn-infused vodka will bring intrigue to a drink like a Bloody Mary. Ginger, the cornerstone of mules and bucks (see chapter 3, pages 79 to 109), offers a warming spice that will tingle your throat, too; it's often a friend to spirits like rum and gin, but it finds a nice corner in Jessi Lorraine's Fixer-Upper (page 167), which pairs a homemade Gingergrass Syrup with whiskey and scotch, using a sour construct. And then there are ingredients like Sichuan or Sansho peppercorns and Buzz Button flowers that, while not outright hot, pique the palate in their own sort of numbing way; we like to use these in concentrated tinctures or syrups, as Caer Maiko Ferguson does in her Red-Crowned Crane (page 160), a Sansho-spiked Paloma riff.

More than Just Tequila

For a long time, it seemed like the only drinks that were getting this fiery treatment were those made with agave spirits. Tequila and mezcal do take heat on in a great way. And we often play with infusing spirits from cultures that have chiles in their cuisine, like pisco from Peru or Chile, say, with aji panca peppers, or Jamaican rum with Scotch bonnet pepper. But there's a place for spice alongside plenty of other spirits, too.

There is no hard fast rule as to what kind of chile goes with what kind of spirit, but in general, we tend to like fresh chiles with the brightness of a clear spirit and dried chiles with the richness of a brown, barrel-aged spirit. Those somewhat mild peppers, like ancho chiles, for example, are more of an ember than a flame and will translate nicely to an aged rum or a drink based in another barrel-aged brown spirit. We've even infused fortified wine—port, specifically—with mulato chiles, which made for an interesting pairing. The dried chiles play on the sweet, rich, raisin-y side of the port.

Go on, see where else you can bring the heat.

DEALER'S CHOICE

Give us PIQUE!
We want the
Caribbean answer
to the call for spicy.

CREATOR

YOLANDA BÁEZ
Speed Rack competitor

---

2 ounces (60 ml) blanco tequila

¾ ounce (22.5 ml) Spicy Syrup (page 262)

¾ ounce (22.5 ml) lemon juice

3 dashes Pique Bitters (page 261)

2 to 3 ounces (60 to 90 ml) Grapefruit, Passion Fruit, Ancho Verde Soda Water (page 260)

½ ounce (15 ml) Fernet Branca

Grapefruit wheel and rosemary sprig, for garnish

VIVA LA VIDA

"Speed Rack has impacted my career in many ways," says Yoli Báez. "One of the most beautiful things is I've had the opportunity to meet people around the country with a passion to do something for a beautiful cause." Having moved from Puerto Rico to Miami about a decade ago, she first heard about Speed Rack while working at the bar Broken Shaker, but she didn't compete until Season 9 when she relocated to New York City. While competing, there's no time to infuse syrups or make DIY bitters or carbonate your own soda, but in making this variation on the Paloma, which gets its spiciness from three different sources, Yoli has done it all. "I wanted to create a spicy, refreshing, tropical cocktail with a bitter touch," she says. If you endeavor to make all the components of this very dynamic drink (it's well worth the effort!), know that the Pique Bitters take two weeks to infuse. If you're short on time, you can sub in Hellfire or Firewater bitters. And conversely, if carbonating soda is your sort of thing, just swap the soda water in this recipe for still and fire up your siphon. (Photo on page 146.)

HOW TO MAKE THE DRINK

Add the tequila, spicy syrup, lemon juice, and bitters to a cocktail shaker filled with ice. Shake until cold and strain into a Collins glass over ice. Top with the grapefruit, passion fruit, ancho verde soda water and float the Fernet on the surface of the drink. Garnish with the grapefruit wheel and rosemary sprig and serve.

CREATOR

YANA VOLFSON
Speed Rack competitor

———

1½ ounces (45 ml) Infusion #1 or #2 (page 260)

¾ ounce (22.5 ml) lime or lemon juice (use lime with #1, lemon with #2)

½ ounce (15 ml) agave nectar

Lime or lemon wheel (use lime with #1, lemon with #2), for garnish

ESL

As the beverage director for chef Enrique Olveras's New York City restaurants, Cosme and Atla, Yana Volfson has been focused on agave spirits for years and has inevitably been forced to spend a portion of that time thinking about spicy margaritas. With dozens of chiles at her fingertips, she's been able to mix and match them in myriad ways. Here, Yana offers up a choose-your-own-adventure recipe for spicy margaritas, with two distinctly different mezcal infusions. One utilizes dried red chiles (which she directed us to "stir and shake and show love to this infusion over time") and is paired with *lime* juice. The other is made from fresh green chiles and paired with *lemon* juice. On paper, a spicy margarita is easy to make, it appears simple, but Yana's two-in-one recipe proves that it's possible to find complexity here. "By layering the chile infusion one can find flavors of spice and not just direct heat or burn," she told us. Yana follows the template for a Tommy's Margarita, a simple (now modern classic) version of a margarita using just tequila, lime, and agave nectar. "Those of us brought up in the public school system might recognize the acronym ESL to read English as a Second Language but I wanted to reclaim power with a new definition: Espadín, Spice, Lime," says Yana. We're all for it.

HOW TO MAKE THE DRINK

Add all the ingredients to a cocktail shaker filled with ice. Shake until cold and strain into a rocks glass over fresh ice. Garnish with the citrus wheel and serve.

INFUSIONS: Firing Up
Spirits and Syrups

ON INFUSING
SPIRITS WITH CHILES

- Start with just a half bottle of spirit—no need to infuse a whole bottle from the jump. Pour the spirit into a pitcher or plastic container.

- Decide how much spice you're going for. Most of the heat comes from the seeds and membranes of the pepper, so including these will further amp up the heat; it's up to you as to whether you keep them or ditch them. We recommend starting with one pepper—chopped not whole—for every 12 ounces (360 ml) of spirit.

- If it's fire you seek—and not so much the vegetal quality of the chile, just use a small amount of the whole pepper and then add only the seeds and membranes from another.

- When infusing dried peppers, toast them in a pan on the stove first in order to soften them and release the oils in the skin.

- Once you've added the peppers to the liquid, set a timer and taste it every 20 minutes. It's hard to really know how much spice a spirit will take on, so this is not a set it and forget it sort of deal; you don't want to leave the pepper in the bottle overnight and walk away. The hotter the pepper, the faster it will infuse.

- Once the spirit has achieved your desired spice level, strain the solids out.

- Store infusions made with fresh peppers in the refrigerator for up to 3 months. Those made with dried chiles can stay at room temperature for up to 3 months.

ON INFUSING
SYRUPS WITH CHILES

- The base syrup can be made with any sugar you'd like: granulated, demerara, agave nectar, etc.

- Because agave spirits are so often the star in spicy drinks, using agave nectar as a base can make for a nice bridge within a cocktail.

- Unlike spirits, syrups don't contain alcohol to extract heat and flavor, so they can often withstand a longer infusion. But taste regularly.

- To get even more of the juicy, vegetal pepper flavor into the syrup, juice some of the peppers and add that to the syrup or agave nectar base.

- Another simple way to infuse is to just blend the chiles right into the simple syrup.

- Chiles are great paired with other warming spices in syrups. Try cinnamon, star anise, or cardamom.

CHOOSING
CHILES

We know that accessibility to certain varieties of chiles may be different all over the world. Much in the same way that you can swap different spirits into recipes, you can substitute other peppers, as well. Maybe you can't take the heat, maybe there aren't chiles de árbol in your market; whatever the case, there's a pepper for that. Here's our guide to the peppers we love by flavor profile, so that you can mix and match depending on what's in your local market or spice shop.

CHILE PEPPER CHEAT SHEET

CHILE	dried / fresh	mild	spicy	very spicy	vegetal	fruity	smoky	earthy	sweet
BANANA PEPPER	FRESH	●							
GREEN BELL PEPPER	FRESH	●			●	●			
RED BELL PEPPER	FRESH	●				●			
POBLANO	FRESH	●			●				
ANCHO	DRIED	●				●	●	●	
JALAPEÑO	FRESH		●		●				
SERRANO	FRESH		●		●	●		●	
CHILE DE ÁRBOL	DRIED		●				●	●	
CHIPOTLE	DRIED		●			●	●	●	●
CALABRIAN	BOTH		●			●	●		
AJI PANCA	DRIED		●			●	●		
AJI AMARILLO	BOTH		●			●			
BIRD'S EYE	FRESH			●		●			
GHOST PEPPER	FRESH			●		●	●	●	●
HABANERO	FRESH			●					
GUAJILLO	DRIED			●			●		●
SCOTCH BONNET	FRESH			●					●

HOT LIPS

Defying one of the most basic tenets of cocktail making, Jessica Gonzalez first made Hot Lips with the goal of creating the ultimate *stirred* citrus drink. At the time, back in 2010, she was bartending at New York City's Death & Co. She took the drink with her when she moved on to The NoMad Bar and, when NoMad opened in London, Hot Lips appeared on that menu, too. In short time, it became an undeniable modern classic. "I don't know that I've credited myself with influencing a specific drink as much as helping to open young bartenders' minds to the technique of stirring citrus in a cocktail. A reminder that rules are made to be broken." With a split base of fiery jalapeño-infused tequila and mezcal, the drink is evened out with lemon and pineapple juices—and not one, but two syrups, a vanilla syrup (use extras in your coffee in the morning!) that brings some warming depth to the drink, and just a teaspoon of cane syrup, which gives the drink its slinky mouthfeel. "Overall, the flavors are simple, but the texture created by stirring this drink makes it feel luxurious," Jessica told us. When infusing the tequila, she advises that it ought to be "very spicy for the best balance." And we are more than okay with that.

CREATOR

JESSICA GONZALEZ
friend of Speed Rack

Fine sea salt, for rim

¾ ounce (22.5 ml) Jalapeño-Infused Tequila (recipe follows)

¾ ounce (22.5 ml) mezcal, preferably Sombra

½ ounce (15 ml) lemon juice

¾ ounce (22.5 ml) pineapple juice

¾ ounce (22.5 ml) Vanilla Syrup (page 262)

1 teaspoon Cane Syrup (page 260)

HOW TO MAKE THE DRINK

Rim a rocks glass with the fine sea salt. Add all the ingredients to a mixing glass filled with ice and stir until cold. Strain into the rocks glass over ice and serve.

Jalapeño-Infused Tequila

Makes about 2 cups (480 ml)

---

3 medium jalapeños, diced

2 cups (480 ml) blanco tequila

Add the jalapeños and tequila to a food-safe container. Let steep for 5 minutes and taste to check the spice level. Steep longer, if necessary, straining out the chiles once your desired spice level has been reached. Pour through a funnel back into the tequila bottle and store in the refrigerator for 2 months.

FROM LEFT TO RIGHT:
Sonámbula (page 156),
Chica en Fuego (page 157),
Hot Lips (page 154)

FROM THE FOUNDERS

Make this for the
spicy margarita lover
in your life.

SONÁMBULA

Sonámbula, which means "sleepwalker" in Spanish, is meant to be a spicy yet calming cocktail. This one is important to me: It was the first drink I ever put on a menu—from the days when I was working at Fort Defiance in Red Hook, Brooklyn, back in 2009. It remains on my menu at Leyenda to this day. I think the word "margarita" has been diluted to mean "anything made with an agave spirit and citrus," but the original specs for the cocktail were that of a classic daisy—made with a liqueur, specifically triple sec. So, technically in my eyes, this isn't a margarita variation but just a delicious, spicy tequila sour.

CREATOR

IVY MIX
Speed Rack co-founder

2 ounces (60 ml) Jalapeño-Infused Tequila (see page 154)

1 ounce (30 ml) lemon juice

¾ ounce (22.5 ml) Chamomile Syrup (recipe follows)

2 dashes Peychaud's bitters

2 dashes mole bitters

Lemon wheel, for garnish

HOW TO MAKE THE DRINK

Add all the ingredients to a cocktail shaker filled with ice. Shake until cold and fine strain into a chilled coupe. Garnish with a lemon wheel and serve.

Chamomile Syrup

Makes about 2½ cups (600ml)

2 bags chamomile tea

2 cups (400 g) granulated sugar

Add 1 cup (240 ml) water to a small pot and bring to a boil. Remove from the heat and add the tea bags, stirring to fully cover with water. Let steep for 15 minutes. Remove the tea bags and return the pot to the stove over low heat. Add the sugar and stir until all the sugar has dissolved; remove from the heat. Store in an airtight container in the refrigerator for up to 1 month.

Make this for your
adventurous friend
seeking something a
little bit spicy and a
little bit sweet.

CHICA EN FUEGO

CREATOR

LYNNETTE MARRERO
Speed Rack co-founder

1½ ounces (45 ml) pisco, preferably Macchu Pisco La Diablada

½ ounce (15 ml) crème de cacao

½ ounce (15 ml) chile liqueur, preferably Ancho Reyes or Xila

¾ ounce (22.5 ml) pineapple juice

½ ounce (15 ml) lemon juice

Shaved dark chocolate, for garnish

This is a cocktail with an agenda. I wanted to change bar-goers' minds about which spirits go with spice. Agave spirits are often the fallback when it comes to spicy drinks—but pisco also works beautifully with chile heat. I originally created this drink for Macchu Pisco, a women-founded brand (it's run by sisters Melanie and Lizzie Asher) and one of the first evangelists of Peruvian pisco to really find a stage in the craft cocktail realm. This particular bottling and blend of grapes was made in honor of their grandmother. For a little intrigue, I added a hit of cacao—chile with chocolate is one of the all-time great pairings. Shake in some citrus and pineapple, and you have a drink that's refreshing, fruity, and subtly spicy—and completely unexpected.

HOW TO MAKE THE DRINK

Add all the ingredients to a cocktail shaker with 2 large ice cubes. Shake just until the ingredients are integrated, then strain into a rocks glass filled with crushed ice. Garnish with the chocolate shavings and serve.

DEALER'S
CHOICE

Take us to the
Yucatán Peninsula!
Give us the feeling
of sand between our
toes with a tequila-
based, fruity long
drink with a kick!

LA FLAMENCA

There's always such an adrenaline rush with the end of every Speed Rack competition, but one of the more memorable exclamation points came at the end of nationals in Season 7, when Mary Palac chopped off her gorgeous locks onstage and donated them to charity. "Speed Rack has been a catalyst for me," says Mary Palac. "It gave me this community of strong, smart, and determined women who at every step of my career have either boosted me up or caught me when I've fallen." We have watched her do the same for so many others over the years. Born in the Philippines, Mary has been a crucial part of the Bay Area bar world for a decade, mentoring and looking out for those who need it. For this book, she made a tropical rendition of the classic tequila-and-grapefruit Paloma (page 257) that is loud, colorful, and JUICY. Knowing that she wanted to bring her tropical heartthrob, passion fruit, into the mix, Mary used the bitterness of Campari as a bridge to the grapefruit juice, with Ancho Reyes Verde bringing a little heat. And she omits the bubbles altogether. "By making [the Paloma] long and shaken instead of fizzy, and adding a touch of spice, the drink is still familiar but something entirely new," she says. Spoken like a woman who's made cocktails on stage under hot lights, she offers this warning: "Don't shake the drink too much since it'll be going over crushed ice!" A lesson well learned.

CREATOR

MARY PALAC
*Speed Rack competitor,
regional winner*

1½ ounces (45 ml) blanco tequila, preferably Espolòn

½ ounce (15 ml) Campari

¼ ounce (7.5 ml) Ancho Reyes Verde

¾ ounce (22.5 ml) lemon juice

¾ ounce (22.5 ml) Passion Fruit Syrup (recipe follows)

4 ounces (120 ml) grapefruit juice

Long grapefruit twist, for garnish

HOW TO MAKE THE DRINK

Add all the ingredients to a cocktail shaker filled with ice. Shake until cold and strain into a Collins or hurricane glass filled with crushed ice. Express the grapefruit twist over the drink, place in the glass, and serve.

Passion Fruit Syrup

Makes about 2 cups (480 ml)

1 cup (8 ounces, 240 ml) frozen passion fruit pulp, thawed (see Resources, page 259)

½ cup (100 g) granulated sugar

Combine all the ingredients in a blender pitcher with ½ cup (120 ml) water. Blend until the sugar is fully dissolved. Store in an airtight container in the refrigerator for up to 2 weeks.

RED-CROWNED CRANE

CREATOR

CAER MAIKO
FERGUSON
Speed Rack competitor

Fine sea salt, for rim

2 ounces (60 ml) sweet potato shochu, like Takara's Honkaku Kurokame

½ ounce (15 ml) lime juice

¼ ounce (7.5 ml) Aperol

½ ounce (15 ml) Sansho Pepper Syrup (recipe follows)

2 ounces (60 ml) soda water, to top

Long grapefruit twist, for garnish

"I am having a lot of fun playing with the traditional spirits of Asia these days: shochu, soju, baijiu, arak. They're underutilized in Western cocktails, so it's fun to play with something that feels very new," says Caer Maiko Ferguson. Shochu is often used in highballs in Japan. (Caer uses one made from sweet potato here for its similarities with the roasted notes found in some agave-based spirits.) She'll swap it in any drink as a tequila replacement. For this Dealer's Choice for the book, the trick was to find the right path to spiciness. She looked to a favored classic, the Paloma (page 257), as a blueprint, adding Aperol to the mix for its grapefruit flavors. Then she brought the heat with a syrup made from crushed sansho, a Japanese pepper that she says is similar to Chinese Szechuan, but with a greener edge. Whereas the Paloma is named for a dove, this is named for a bird that's native to Japan. Even the appearance of the drink recalls the bird's plumage, Caer says: "The white salt rim and the red orange tone of the Aperol are reminiscent of the crane's coloring, with the long grapefruit twist alluding to the long neck of a crane."

HOW TO MAKE THE DRINK

Salt the rim of a Collins glass. Add the shochu, lime juice, Aperol, and sansho syrup to a cocktail shaker filled with ice. Shake until cold and strain into the glass over fresh ice. Top with soda water, garnish with the grapefruit twist, and serve.

Sansho Pepper Syrup

Makes about 1½ cups (360 ml)

1 cup (200 g) granulated sugar

1 cup (240 ml) hot water

1 tablespoon sansho pepper, crushed (see Resources, page 259)

Combine all the ingredients in a heat-safe container. Stir until incorporated. Let sit for 20 to 30 minutes. Strain through a coffee filter or other tightly woven strainer. Store in an airtight container in the refrigerator for up to 1 month.

It's brunch and we
want to have a drink
that packs a little
heat with our eggs.
Can you make us a
spicy savory drink?

BUFFALO SOLDIER

"One of the best days of my life was when I won the Speed Rack Puerto Rico competition and got to share that very special moment with my friends and family," says Gigi Temprano, a fixture behind the bar at Old San Juan's La Factoría, which has been ranked one of the World's 50 Best Bars for five years running, no doubt thanks to Gigi's contributions. Incredibly athletically inclined, Gigi tackled Speed Rack with the same regimented approach. And when she moved on to the nationals in New Orleans, she was six months pregnant with her daughter—a true family affair. Gigi's Buffalo Soldier is her gin-based take on a spicy margarita, but rather than infusing the gin with chiles or adding heat via a tincture or syrup, she dashes in a little bit of vinegary Buffalo-style hot sauce, bringing an extra tang to this surprisingly refreshing yet fiery drink. Many drinks at La Factoría are made using a house lemon-lime mix, and she applies that here—it's simply equal parts lemon and lime juice blended together.

CREATOR

GENEVIEVE "GIGI" TEMPRANO
Speed Rack Puerto Rico competitor, national winner

2 ounces (60 ml) gin

½ ounce (15 ml) orange liqueur, preferably Cointreau

¾ ounce (22.5 ml) grapefruit juice

½ ounce (15 ml) lemon-lime juice blend

½ ounce (15 ml) Simple Syrup (page 262)

2 to 3 dashes Buffalo-style hot sauce

Orange wheel, for garnish (optional)

HOW TO MAKE THE DRINK

Add all the ingredients to a cocktail shaker filled with ice. Shake until cold and strain into a highball glass over fresh ice. Garnish with an orange wheel, if using, and serve.

DEALER'S
CHOICE

Can we get a spice-
driven gin drink?
Stirred and up, please.

MY NAME IS NOBODY

CREATOR

BECKALY FRANKS
Speed Rack competitor

¾ ounce (22.5 ml) Ancho
Reyes Original chile liqueur

¾ ounce (22.5 ml) gin

¾ ounce (22.5 ml) sweet
vermouth

¾ ounce (22.5 ml) Aperol

Grapefruit swath, for
garnish

Beckaly Franks is a true rock star—an artist with a strong point of view.
She competed in the first three seasons of Speed Rack (including one
in full-on Ziggy Stardust makeup), representing Portland, Oregon, and
then lit off for Hong Kong, where she's lived since 2015 and co-owns a
handful of bars, including the Pontiac, a staple of Asia's 50 Best Bars
list. Calling this drink one of her "personal modern classics," in Beckaly's hands the Negroni finds its fire. "Often when someone wants a
spicy drink the automatic go-to is a spicy margarita; you need the acid
and sugar to love on that spice." But in a Negroni, Beckaly uses sweet
vermouth as what she describes as the sugary "cushion" along with the
bitterness of Aperol for a true balancing act. For the garnish, Beckaly
pulls a wide, long strip of grapefruit peel, called a swath, for a big citrusy inflection just as you're about to sip the drink.

HOW TO MAKE THE DRINK

Add all the ingredients to a mixing glass filled with ice. Stir until cold and

strain into a chilled cocktail glass. Express the grapefruit swath over the top

of the drink and place it in the glass. Serve.

FIXER-UPPER

CREATOR

JESSI LORRAINE
Speed Rack competitor, regional winner

1½ ounces (45 ml) wheated whiskey, preferably Starward Two-Fold Double Grain

½ ounce (15 ml) Islay single-malt scotch, preferably Laphroaig 10-Year-Old

¾ ounce (22.5 ml) lemon juice

¾ ounce (22.5 ml) Honey Syrup (page 260)

¾ ounce (22.5 ml) Gingergrass Syrup (recipe follows)

Angostura bitters and a lemon twist, for garnish

"Growing up in the beverage industry, I never felt respected or taken seriously by men," says Jessi Lorraine. "So, when I heard about the possibility of being a part of a women-powered event and getting to network with such strong, brilliant women in the industry, it was a no-brainer." Jessi is the first person we remember showing up to Speed Rack as if she were off to Comic-Con—in full pink Power Ranger regalia. She competed (and won) and has been with us for the long haul, mentoring emerging Speed Rackers in San Francisco and now in Los Angeles. For this Dealer's Choice, Jessi Lorraine used a modern classic as a starting point, the Penicillin (page 257), which gets its heat not from chiles, but from fresh ginger. Jessi combines two whiskies just as the original does: a wine barrel–aged Australian one, matched with smoky Laphroaig scotch, and she brings the drink added dimension with her signature syrup made from ginger and lemongrass. (Use any extra syrup for a next-level Tom Collins.) "Whenever prompted to put together a cocktail quickly, I always like to tap into my arsenal of flavor pairings. I love the way turmeric, lemongrass, and ginger play with the baking spice notes of Angostura bitters," she says.

HOW TO MAKE THE DRINK

Add all the ingredients to a cocktail shaker filled with ice. Shake until cold and double strain into a large rocks glass filled with ice. Float 5 to 7 dashes Angostura bitters on top of the drink. Express the lemon twist over the drink, place it in the glass, and serve.

Gingergrass Syrup

Makes 12 ounces (360 ml)

½ stalk fresh lemongrass

1½ teaspoons ground turmeric

2½ cups (250 g) roughly chopped fresh ginger

1¼ cups (250 g) granulated sugar

Using a mallet or a rolling pin, pound the lemongrass to soften it, and give it a rough chop. Combine the lemongrass, turmeric, and 1 cup (240 ml) water in a saucepan over medium heat and bring it to a boil. Reduce to a simmer and cook for 5 minutes. While still hot, carefully fine strain the liquid into a blender pitcher or food processor and add the chopped ginger and sugar. Blend until combined and cool to room temperature. Fine strain into an airtight container. Store in the refrigerator for up to 2 weeks. This syrup tends to separate, so give it a good shake before using it.

Make this for anyone
in the mood for a
smoky old-fashioned
with a kick.

CREATOR

LYNNETTE
MARRERO
Speed Rack co-founder

1½ ounces (45 ml) blended
scotch, preferably
Buchanan's

½ ounce (15 ml) mezcal

¼ ounce (7.5 ml) Chile-
Cinnamon Syrup (recipe
follows)

2 dashes Bittermens Mole
bitters

1 teaspoon edible
glitter (optional but
recommended!; see
Resources, page 259)

Orange twist and cinnamon
stick (optional), for garnish

PLAN AHEAD

GLITTER REVOLUTION

I created this cocktail to honor the women of Mexico City's "revolución
diamantina," or glitter revolution. In the summer of 2019, thousands
took to the streets to protest sexual violence against women, spurred
by the horrific assault of a teen girl by Mexican police. The protest
movement got its name when women showered CDMX's security chief
with pink glitter at their inaugural demonstration on August 12. Scotch
is very popular in Latin America—especially blended Scotch. It finds
itself at every celebration. I wanted to take something that has been
traditionally gendered as male and liberate it from those limitations.
To give the drink a kick, I make a chile-cinnamon syrup made with a
mix of dried chiles de árbol, fresh jalapeños, and ground cayenne pepper. The cinnamon becomes a sort of gentle introduction between the
tingling spice of the cayenne and the warmth of the scotch. This syrup
takes about 4 hours to make; plan accordingly. You can use any excess
syrup to spice up margaritas, daiquiris, and other sours.

HOW TO MAKE THE DRINK

Add all the ingredients to a mixing glass filled with ice and stir until cold.
Strain into a double old-fashioned glass over a large ice cube. Express the
orange twist over the drink and place it in the glass. If you'd like some extra
flair, hold one end of a cinnamon stick over a flame until it begins to smoke.
Place the cinnamon stick (smoking end up) in the drink, and serve.

Chile-Cinnamon Syrup

Makes about ¾ cup (180 ml)

½ cup (100 g) granulated
sugar

2 cinnamon sticks, broken
into pieces

1 dried chile de árbol, cut
into pieces

2 slices fresh jalapeño

1 dash cayenne pepper, or
more, to taste

Combine the sugar
and cinnamon with ½
cup (120 ml) water in
a small saucepan and
bring to a boil over high
heat. Reduce the heat
to low and simmer for
a few minutes, just until
the sugar is dissolved.

Remove from the heat,
cover, and let stand
for 4 hours. In the last
30 minutes, add the
chile de árbol, jalapeño,
and cayenne, and stir.
When the syrup reaches
your desired heat level,
strain it into an airtight

container and store in
the refrigerator for up to
3 weeks.

The effervescent Kaslyn Bos celebrates her win at the Northeast regional in Season 11 in NYC.

WHAT'S YOUR LIQUID GUILTY PLEASURE?

"Lime-A-Ritas. (Ridiculous, right?)"
—NATALIE FRAZIER

"Rumple Minze! I know plenty of
people think it's disgusting, but
it's like drinking mouthwash—in

"Mango White Claws . . . yup."
—CLARA NOBLE

"Bud Light Orange. It's so bad, but
so good! I add a dash of Ango when
I'm feeling fancy."

"Fruity margaritas. Put berries with
my tequila any day."
—CAER MAIKO FERGUSON

"I do love a pickleback. I straight up
drink the juice from the jar!"

DEALER'S CHOICE

Give us a savory, peppery martini.

HANG ON LITTLE TOMATO

CREATOR

ELYSE BLECHMAN
*Speed Rack competitor,
regional winner*

1½ ounces (45 ml) Roasted Garlic and Pepper–Infused Vodka (page 261)

½ ounce (15 ml) dry vermouth, preferably Dolin, or fino sherry

1 ounce (30 ml) Tomato Water (recipe follows)

Skewered cherry tomato, halved and salted

Without a doubt, Elyse Blechman forever changed Speed Rack. For the first few seasons, competitors would complete their round and maybe start jumping up and down or giving high fives to people in the crowd while their opponent finished theirs, but during Season 5, in Houston, Elyse garnished her drinks, smacked the buzzer, and turned around and cheered on Zulco Rodríguez, her opponent. We get chills just thinking about it. And we have seen this kind of selfless support spread around the globe throughout the years; it's the best, the pinnacle of our mantra that rising tides float all boats. For this Dealer's Choice, Elyse created a martini–meets–Bloody Mary that combines a peppery-infused vodka (a recipe from Death & Co.'s first book) with an herbal, savory tomato water devised by greenmarket guru and Gramercy Tavern chef Michael Anthony. It's a drink best made in peak summer when your garden is overflowing with beefsteak tomatoes and perfumy basil.

HOW TO MAKE THE DRINK

Add all the ingredients to a mixing glass filled with ice. Stir until cold and strain into a chilled coupe. Garnish with the cherry tomato skewer and serve.

Tomato Water

Makes about 1½ cups (360 ml)

Recipe by chef Michael Anthony, first published in *Bon Appétit* (August 2013)

2 to 3 beefsteak tomatoes (about 12 ounces/340 g)

½ cup (20 g) fresh basil leaves

¼ cup (10 g) fresh cilantro

¼ cup (13 g) fresh flat-leaf parsley

1 medium shallot

1 clove garlic

1½ tablespoons white wine vinegar

1½ teaspoons kosher salt

Add all the ingredients to a blender or food processor and pulse until coarsely chopped and combined. Strain through a fine-mesh sieve lined with several layers of cheesecloth into a food-safe container. Cover, without pressing on the solids. Place in the refrigerator to continue straining and chill overnight. Store the resulting tomato water in an airtight container in the refrigerator for up to 3 days.

RED BOTTOM STILETTO

Gia St. George Terry is one of our Speed Rackers who came to us for the charity aspect. Her grandmother survived stage 4 breast cancer. Almost as if on a dare, Gia infused a syrup with ghost pepper (aptly named for its haunting heat) for this variation on a Stiletto, a drink usually made with whiskey, cranberry juice, amaretto, and lemon. "I wanted to use something completely different from jalapeños or serranos," she says. Ghost pepper is very rarely found in cocktails because it is so potent (wear gloves), but Gia found a way to work with it, surprising even herself! "I paired the ghost pepper with cinnamon to help mask the bite. It ended up being the most wonderful pairing." This is added to spicy rye whiskey, a muddled strawberry, and the bitter aperitif Byrrh Grand Quinquina. "This cocktail is super sexy, sultry, smooth with a tease of heat—like a fiery red stiletto heel on a night out," she says.

CREATOR

GIA ST. GEORGE TERRY
Speed Rack competitor

---

1 strawberry, destemmed and sliced in half

1½ ounces (45 ml) rye whiskey, preferably Rittenhouse

½ ounce (15 ml) Byrrh Grand Quinquina aperitif

¾ ounce (22.5 ml) lemon juice

¾ ounce (22.5 ml) Cinnamon–Ghost Pepper Syrup (recipe follows)

Strawberry slice, for garnish

HOW TO MAKE THE DRINK

Add the halved strawberry to a cocktail shaker and muddle. Add the other ingredients and fill the shaker with ice. Shake until cold and double strain into a Collins glass filled with crushed ice. Garnish with the strawberry slice and serve.

Cinnamon–Ghost Pepper Syrup

Makes about 2½ cups (600 ml)

3 long cinnamon sticks

½ whole dried ghost pepper

1½ cups (300 g) granulated sugar

Combine all the ingredients in a saucepan with 1½ cups (360 ml) water and bring to a boil over medium heat. Remove from the heat and let the syrup steep overnight. Strain into an airtight container and store in the refrigerator for up to 2 weeks.

Natasha Bermudez pours her version of a 50/50 Gibson, the Kobayashi Martini (page 180).

CHAPTER 6

CRYSTAL CLEAR

MASTERING THE MARTINI

The martini is, without doubt, the most iconic cocktail in the world, and everyone has their own highly specific opinions about it. For some, it's a balance of gin and vermouth, stirred until ice cold, and garnished with a lemon twist. Others clench their vodka bottle and make a meal out of it with blue-cheese stuffed olives. For others, a martini must be dirty as can be, with just as much cloudy olive brine as spirit. Ivy likes her martinis pretty wet with a dry vermouth that carries a lot of acidity, like the one from Lo-Fi, and Lynnette, too, takes hers with ample vermouth either as a 2:1 or 50/50. We both drink

them in the self-proclaimed "grandma-style" with an olive *and* a twist.

And then, of course there are the vermouth haters, a group we cannot possibly understand. And since we're on the subject, keep your vermouth—any fortified wine, actually—in the fridge! We'd shout this from the rooftops, if we could! Perhaps the reason so many people have this bizarre vermouth phobia is that they're drinking dead vermouth. Would you drink a glass of white wine from a bottle that has been open and sitting on a shelf for a year? No, probably not. Don't do it with vermouth.

It will last about three months in the fridge before it starts to lose its aromas and flavors.

Not nearly as contentious, but more than deserving of attention, are the other members of the classic martini family, including the Gibson (page 201), which is served with a pickled pearl onion; the Vesper a mostly-gin iteration with an ounce of vodka; or the Martinez, a drink that subs in sweet vermouth and adds a splash of maraschino liqueur. The Astoria, created in the 1930s at New York City's Waldorf Astoria hotel, was an ahead-of-its-time reverse martini, with more than three times as much vermouth as gin, a trend we see many a Speed Rack bartender embracing for a little bit of temperance. Each of these drinks has its own time and place and is a good jumping-off point for Dealer's Choice scenarios.

Classic cocktail books will tell you that a martini is 2 parts gin to 1 part vermouth, but flipping through this chapter, it becomes very clear that no one's held to these specs. Today's bartenders are swapping out all of the elements in the martini from bitters to brine to the fortified wine.

But know that this chapter does not dabble in the "other martinis" that composed whole menus in the 1990s. Those, like the Porn Star Martini or the chocolate martini, are really only martinis in name; all they have in common with the classic is that they're served up in the same iconic glass. We make exceptions for a handful of espresso martini variations in chapter 8 and a serious take on an apple martini, the Snap Apple Pop (page 197) from Miranda Breedlove, that incorporates *real* apples in a variety of ways—and tastes nothing like a green apple Jolly Rancher.

The Mechanics of a Martini

There are some techniques that will improve your martini game no matter your preferences. One thing we (not to mention our Speed Rack judges) are sticklers about when it comes to martinis is dilution—difficult to master in the best of conditions, let alone under the hot lights of the stage! It's where we often see the biggest user error and it's the most important part of this cocktail.

Understandably, ideal dilution is a tricky thing to teach; knowing if a martini is cold enough is checked easily enough by feeling the outside of the mixing glass, but dilution is something that we *taste* for. The mission is to have all the ingredients meld together, without losing their oomph.

Traditionally, a martini is stirred. This style of cocktail is meant to be silky, with as little air integrated into the drink as possible. With the revolutions of ice in the mixing glass, you're coaxing the ingredients to get along and become one, rather than forcing them to do so by shaking. Think silky smooth rather than plush velvet.

If you over-stir or if your ice is not up to snuff and melts quickly, the drink will never be what it should be. So, set yourself up for success. The best-case scenario is that you're starting with ingredients that are already cold. Keep your gin or vodka in the freezer and all fortified wines in the fridge. With no other category of drinks is chilling your glass so important; don't sacrifice that hard-won chill. We recommend using 1¼-inch (3 cm) cubed ice (see page 21) for making most drinks, but here it will make all the difference, as the cubes melt slowly and consistently. If all you have on hand is that weird crescent-shaped ice that your freezer makes, it will melt very quickly, so use much less. Sometimes you can get away with using just a couple of those crummy cubes and stirring them until they've fully melted.

Our favorite (and most consistent) way to ensure ideal dilution is to batch out martinis, add ¾ or 1 ounce (22.5 or 30 ml) water per drink, and put them in a bottle in the freezer to get frosty before serving. This way, you don't have to worry about over/under doing it and you'll have a martini at the ready whenever you need one. Just give it a stir and pour it in a glass.

Of course, the question of which glass to use is always a conversation when it comes to martinis. We're seeing the tricky-to-carry, but chic-as-hell v-shaped martini glass making a serious comeback, but they're also great in a coupe or a Nick & Nora or other stemmed cocktail glass.

Beyond Gin and Vodka

When it comes to choosing a base spirit, the world of gin is vast. London Dry gins are a favorite and tend to be assertively piney with a healthy dose of juniper, but there are plenty of other styles that veer in the directions of citrus or floral. Vodka martinis became trendy in the sixties in the era of three martini lunches and the slogan "vodka leaves you breathless." Today, some snooty bartenders will say that vodka doesn't deserve vermouth; we say drink what you want. There's no hard-and-fast rule that says an agave-based spirit, like tequila or mezcal, or a grape-based spirit, like pisco, can't serve as the base.

The possibilities when it comes to vermouth may well exceed gin! And as the 50/50 martini has become more and more popular, the conversation surrounding which fortified wine to use becomes livelier. Every country seems to have their own style of vermouth and there are ever more landing on these shores from Spain, Italy, France, and South America. The standard for martinis has long been dry vermouth, usually in the French style, but many are replacing this with blanc/bianco vermouth, which tends to be a bit sweeter and gives more weight to the drink. But there's so much room to play; we love seeing how fortified wines, like salty fino and manzanilla sherries, can bring a savoriness to the equation; the French gentian-based Salers gives an herbal bitterness and quinquinas, made with cinchona bark, will deliver an earthy sweetness. Natasha Bermudez takes her Kobayashi Martini (page 180) to a whole new realm by bringing in both sake and fino sherry.

Also in the martini toolbox are bitters, which will add a little nuance to your drink. Orange bitters are traditional (they pluck the citrus and floral chords of the vermouth in a beautiful way) but today there are so many options. A dash of celery, grapefruit, or even lavender bitters can really change up the game, with no fuss.

Garnish Garden

Finally, whereas garnishes in many styles of cocktails are just there for looks, the simplicity of a martini makes it a very good canvas for flavorful garnishes. Various citrus twists and varieties of olives are easily switched in depending on the profile of the drink you're aiming to highlight. But as with a Gibson (page 201) that's garnished with a teeny pickled onion, we've seen all sorts of farmstand vegetables—tomatillos, cauliflower, radishes, carrots, beets—get the pickle treatment and perk up a martini. Shop the olive bar at the grocery store and get creative.

She's beauty, she's grace, and she's not going anywhere. Here's to the martini and the endless combinations she can embody, as shown in the wide-ranging recipes that follow here.

DEALER'S CHOICE

Make us a reverse
lower-proof martini
with sake and/or
shochu.

KOBAYASHI MARTINI

CREATOR

NATASHA BERMUDEZ
*Speed Rack competitor,
regional winner*

¾ ounce (22.5 ml) sake,
preferably Taru

¾ ounce (22.5 ml) gin,
preferably Roku

¾ ounce (22.5 ml) blanc
vermouth

¾ ounce (22.5 ml) fino
sherry

Cocktail onion, for garnish

"Sake and fortified ingredients can often get overlooked, but they are very versatile when making low-proof cocktails," says Natasha Bermudez. This 50/50 take on a Gibson is equal parts sake and Japanese gin with equal parts blanc vermouth and fino sherry (photo on page 176). Whereas a traditional gin-heavy, full-proof martini might require a good bit of stirring to achieve proper dilution and temperature, "most of the ingredients in this drink will dilute quicker," cautions Natasha. Chill your glass and taste frequently to land the drink where you want it.

HOW TO MAKE THE DRINK

Add the sake, gin, vermouth, and sherry to a mixing glass over ice. Stir until cold and strain into a chilled coupe or Nick & Nora glass. Garnish with the onion and serve.

WHAT'S YOUR FAVORITE CLASSIC COCKTAIL?

"I love a good Hanky Panky. It's one of very few remaining classic cocktails that is known for being developed by a woman bartender."

—JESSI POLLAK

"Paper Plane. Equal parts cocktails are always my favorite. Four unusual ingredients making a perfectly balanced combination."

—FABIANA PINILLOS

"I'm supposed to choose just one?! I guess I go back and forth between a Caipirinha and a London Calling. For me the Caipirinha is the most refreshing drink on a hot day, and I'm pretty much a sucker for anything with gin and fino sherry so the London Calling nails that."

—TESS ANNE SAWYER

"A daiquiri, for sure. Refreshing and crushable at its core and so easily malleable by just slightly tweaking the build or using a blend of rums or a flavored syrup."

—ERIN HAYES

"The Bamboo. I love that it is low ABV and combines my two favorite things: sherry and vermouth!"

—LEANNE FAVRE

"If you're having a bad day and you want a bright and bracing cocktail to perk you up, the Champs-Élysées is a definite go-to."

—PRISCILLA LEONG

"My favorite classic cocktail is a Royal Bermuda Yacht Club. Everyone loves a daiquiri, but it's taken up a notch with a bit of falernum and triple sec. I like to add a touch of rich cane syrup and a dash of tiki bitters for extra flair; I'm annoying like that."

—JILLIAN VOSE

"Brandy Crusta. It is delicious, refreshing, and made with cognac."

—EZRA STAR

"A Queen's Park Swizzle. It is bright and fresh but has a depth of flavor from the bitters on top. They're infinitely modifiable with the use of different styles of rum. It is also super challenging to make beautiful, balanced, and quickly onstage. It is something I focused a lot of attention on because it is seemingly simple, but it is actually quite complex."

—SARAH TROXELL

"I will never say no to a margarita. For me it's the perfect combination of spirit, sugar, and citrus."

—KAITLYN STEWART

"Half and half very dirty vodka martini. Socially acceptable excuse to drink a liquified olive."

—MILLIE TANG

"The Martinez, for me it's not only delicious but it takes me right back to the first time I had one at Arnaud's French 75 Bar."

—JENA ELLENWOOD

"I'm a moody drinker but if I had to pick one it would be a wet gin martini with olives and a twist because when I begin with one, I know it's going to be a fun night."

—YANA VOLFSON

"Classic gimlet because it's pink and delicious!"

—GIGI TEMPRANO

"Adonis! Fortified life is the best life!"

—ANGEL TETA

We would like the
cleanest, sharpest-
yet-nuanced Vesper
you have. A little fruit
could go a long way!

CREATOR

ALEX JUMP
*Speed Rack competitor,
regional winner*

1¼ ounces (37.5 ml) gin,
preferably Old Raj

1 ounce (30 ml) cream
sherry, preferably Alvear
Pale

½ ounce (15 ml) pommeau,
preferably Rhine Hall La
Normande

¼ ounce (7.5 ml) pear
brandy, preferably Clear
Creek

½ dash celery bitters

Lemon twist, for garnish

BORROWED TIME

Plenty of bartenders will tell you that competing in Speed Rack played a role in their career, but for Alex Jump, Speed Rack basically wound up being an audition for a job she'd have less than a year later. When she took the stage in Denver in Season 6, one of the judges was Alex Day, who was on the hunt for a lead bartender to run his new Death & Co. in the Mile High City. She went on to run the bar for four years. The classic Vesper recipe (page 256), one popularized by its appearance in a James Bond film, *Casino Royale*, is not messing around. Often with eight times the amount of gin as vermouth and always with an ounce or so of vodka, as well, it's a big, no-joke drink. Here, Alex opts for something a little lower octane and more complex flavor-wise, essentially concocting a 50/50 martini. "I decided to stick to my favorite martini spec for this drink, keeping it 1½ ounces of full-proof spirit and 1½ ounces of fortified wine/lower-proof spirit. I just think that that style of drink is more enjoyable," she says. Borrowed Time adds up to a balance of aromatic gin and cream sherry, with apple pommeau (a blend of aged apple brandy and fresh apple cider), pear brandy, and savory celery bitters. It's what Alex calls a "juicy, wintery martini." In the words of James Bond, "Once you've tasted it, that's all you want to drink."

HOW TO MAKE THE DRINK

Add all the ingredients to a mixing glass and add ice. Stir until cold and strain into a chilled Nick & Nora glass. Express the lemon twist over the drink, place it in the glass, and serve.

CREATOR

LYNNETTE MARRERO
Speed Rack co-founder

¾ ounce (22.5 ml) reposado tequila

¾ ounce (22.5 ml) pisco, preferably Capurro Acholado

¾ ounce (22.5 ml) Cocchi Americano bianco aperitivo

¾ ounce (22.5 ml) dry vermouth, preferably Dolin

Lemon twist, for garnish

EL CHAPO

A good stiff drink with a strong name to match, this cocktail was a collaborative effort between Jess Gonzalez (see page 154) and me back in 2015 when we were working on a cocktail menu together. With the idea of creating a Latin American Vesper in mind, we eventually wound up with something that is more of a hybrid with a 50/50 martini, with reposado tequila bringing some delicate aged notes and aromatic pisco standing in for gin. I like to use the single-estate Capurro Acholado pisco in this drink because it is a very robust pisco with the perfect balance of aromatics and texture. As a bonus, it's made by a female distiller who took over the distillery from her grandfather. This cocktail is all about capturing those aromas and flavors, which are supported by bitter Cocchi Americano and dry vermouth for a drier finish. It's a drink that makes a great bottled batched drink to keep in the freezer (see page 76 for the how-to). Stir, strain, and enjoy.

HOW TO MAKE THE DRINK

Add all the ingredients to a mixing glass filled with ice. Stir and strain into a chilled Nick & Nora glass. Express the lemon twist over the drink and place it in the glass; serve.

FROM THE
FOUNDERS
———
Make this for the dirty
martini lover who
likes a little fruit with
their savory sips.

CREATOR

IVY MIX
Speed Rack co-founder

1 ounce (30 ml) mango brandy, preferably Rhine Hall

¾ ounce (22.5 ml) gin, preferably Gin Mare

¼ ounce (7.5 ml) white rum, preferably Wray & Nephew Overproof

¾ ounce (22.5 ml) manzanilla sherry, preferably Lustau

½ ounce (15 ml) quinquina blanc, preferably L.N. Mattei Cap Corse Blanc

½ teaspoon apple cider vinegar

Grapefruit twist, for garnish

SUNSHOWERS

Cocktail geeks might roll their eyes at a call for a dirty martini, but I am a big fan. The thing is, I always want to put pinches of salt into my cocktails; nine times out of ten, a little salinity makes the flavors of a cocktail sing louder. So, the saltiness of dirty martinis is my love language. This drink is named after and inspired by the MIA song "Sunshowers," which has a lyric touting salt-and-peppered mangoes. Loving salt—and loving mangos—more than all else, I took the challenge in martini format, beginning with a mango brandy base. There are quite a few mango brandies out there, ranging from light and clean to dense and oily. I like the one from Rhine Hall, a distillery in Chicago, because it's very pure in its fruit notes. Oaxacan mango brandies, which I also love, will add a great deal more funk—not bad just different! When split with gin and combined with sherry and quinquina blanc, the result is a salty, fruity martini to enjoy anywhere, but by a beach would be my first choice!

HOW TO MAKE THE DRINK

Add all the ingredients to a mixing glass filled with ice. Stir until cold and strain into a chilled cocktail glass. Express the grapefruit twist over the drink, place it in the glass, and serve.

CREATOR

DAPHNEE VARY DESHAIES
Speed Rack competitor

1½ ounces (45 ml) single malt scotch, preferably something with salinity, like Talisker 10

¾ ounce (22.5 ml) dry vermouth

¾ ounce (22.5 ml) bianco vermouth

¼ ounce (7.5 ml) pickled ginger brine

A slice of pickled ginger and a smoked Cerignola olive on a pick, for garnish

FUNKY MARTINI FOR HJRONEY

"Hjroney is my wife," says Daphnee Vary Deshaies. "She has an outstanding palate and is one of the pickiest martini drinkers out there. She loves it extra dry and filthy dirty, which I find difficult to balance because it hurts my taste buds every time. I still do it, of course. No judgment there." After experimenting with numerous iterations, this is the martini that stuck. As Hjroney is a scotch lover, Daphnee used salty, smoky Talisker as her base and added vermouth—both dry and bianco (aka blanc in French)—to smooth its sharp edges. Rather than using olive brine to dirty up this martini, she poured in just ¼ ounce (7.5 ml) of pickled ginger brine, garnishing with a slice of the ginger and a salty, smoky green Cerignola to boot. "Wifey LOVES her olives. And this martini was for her," says Daphnee. We love this love and the wild concoction that came from it, made with one person's tastes in mind—a bona fide Dealer's Choice.

HOW TO MAKE THE DRINK

Add all the ingredients to a mixing glass filled with ice. Stir until cold and strain into a chilled martini glass. Garnish with the pickled ginger and olive and serve.

MODERN
CLASSIC

———

A game-changing
50/50 martini with a
peak summer vibe.

CREATOR

JULIE REINER
*Speed Rack mentor and
judge*

1½ ounces (45 ml) gin,
preferably Plymouth

1½ ounces (45 ml) bianco
vermouth, preferably
Martini & Rossi

¾ ounce (22.5 ml) apricot
eau de vie, preferably
Blume Marillen

2 dashes orange bitters

Orange twist, for garnish

GIN BLOSSOM

It's fair to say that Speed Rack wouldn't exist without Julie Reiner. She
has been a boss and a mentor to both of us at various stages of our
careers. She has championed Speed Rack since we started and judged
more times than anyone can count. And when it comes to women who
have shaped the bar world and made inroads for women all along the
way, there's just no one who compares to Julie. Such a legend obviously
has numerous modern classics to her name, but the Gin Blossom is one
of our favorites. Julie created this drink at her Flatiron Lounge while
concepting the cocktail menu for her bar Clover Club in Brooklyn back
in 2008. "It's like a 50/50 martini meets a Perfect Martini," she says,
noting that the bianco vermouth is cut with a little apricot eau de vie.
In fact, it was the Blume Marillen apricot eau de vie that inspired the
drink. Eric Seed, owner of spirits importer Haus Alpenz, brought both
it and an apricot liqueur for her to taste. Of that tasting, the Gin Blossom
and the Slope (a Manhattan variation utilizing the liqueur) were born.
Both cocktails remain on the Clover Club menu fifteen years later and
can be seen on other menus the world over.

HOW TO MAKE THE DRINK

Add all the ingredients to a mixing glass filled with ice. Stir until cold and
strain into a chilled coupe. Express the orange twist over the drink and place
it in the glass; serve.

CREATOR

JESS POMERANTZ
Speed Rack competitor, regional winner, redemption winner

---

2 ounces (60 ml) fino sherry, preferably Lustau

1 ounce (30 ml) blanco vermouth, preferably Lustau Vermut Blanco

2 dashes Bittermens Hopped Grapefruit bitters

1 pinch salt

Grapefruit twist, for garnish

MORTAL SIN

When faced with a Dealer's Choice call for a salty, sherry-inflected martini, Jess Pomerantz says her brain immediately went to an old-school Bamboo (page 258). "It is one of those classics that has such a simple build, but with the right ingredients, it can become such a complex cocktail!" she says. The original Bamboo is composed of equal parts sherry and dry vermouth, but modern bartenders have taken this in many new directions as the popularity (and accessibility) of sherry has increased. And it's not uncommon to see a little sugar added for texture, but here, Jess leans into the classic drink, swapping blanc vermouth for dry, which brings its own sweetness and a little body to the equation. To gild the lily, Jess adds a pinch of salt and a couple dashes of hopped grapefruit bitters. The name of this drink is an ode to Clara Campoamor, borrowing the title of her treatise on voting rights. Jess says Clara "was a twentieth-century Spanish lawyer, politician, and committed suffragette who left her political party" because it opposed women's rights. Campoamor was exiled to Switzerland after speaking out against the Catholic Church early on during the Spanish Civil War. Salty for sure!

HOW TO MAKE THE DRINK

Add all the ingredients to a mixing glass filled with ice. Stir for only 10 to 15 rotations so as not to over dilute and then strain into a chilled cocktail glass. Express the grapefruit twist over the drink and place it in the glass. Serve.

TRANSPARENT GREEN TEA MARTINI

CREATOR

SUMMER LO
Speed Rack competitor, Asia winner

1 ounce (30 ml) Green Tea Hydrosol (recipe follows)

2½ ounces (75 ml) London Dry gin, chilled in the freezer

Lemon twist, for garnish

Summer Lo was our first-ever Speed Rack winner in our Asia competition. And at the Four Seasons in Hong Kong, Summer Lo has found a following for her diamond-clear martinis. The hotel collaborated with Australian distillery Never Never to make a gin just for its Argo bar and there, it's always pulled straight from the freezer and served shockingly, wonderfully cold. "The name Hong Kong literally means 'the harbor that smells good,' which comes from the famous spice and tea leaf trading that happened there," she told us. Summer often uses a rotary evaporator (aka rotovap) to infuse flavors into gin for vermouth-less martinis. Since not many of us have a rotovap hanging around at home, she's concocted a more simplistic recipe for us here, using a hydrosol (water infused with essential oils) made from green tea extract and bergamot. Keep your gin in the freezer, she advises.

HOW TO MAKE THE DRINK

Add the green tea hydrosol to a chilled martini glass. Add the chilled gin. Express the lemon twist over the drink and place it in the glass. Serve.

Green Tea Hydrosol

Makes 8 ounces (240 ml)

6 drops green tea extract (see Resources, page 259)

4 drops bergamot essential oil (see Resources, page 259)

8 ounces (250 ml) boiling water

Add the green tea extract and the bergamot essential oil to the boiling water in a heatproof bowl. Cover the bowl tightly and let it sit for 30 minutes. Pour the mixture through a coffee filter into an airtight container and allow to cool fully before storing the hydrosol in the refrigerator. It will keep indefinitely.

We'd love a slightly
smoky yet still crisp
and bracing martini.

CREATOR

LEANNE FAVRE
Speed Rack competitor

---

2 ounces (60 ml) mezcal,
preferably Los Vecinos

1 ounce (30 ml) white
verjus, preferably Wölffer
Estate

½ ounce (15 ml) Lustau
Vermut Rosé

½ ounce (15 ml) orange
liqueur, preferably
Cointreau

¼ ounce (7.5 ml) Giffard
Rhubarbe liqueur

Orange twist and a food-
safe orchid (optional), for
garnish

BESITO

"My favorite base spirit to mix with is mezcal," says Leanne Favre. "I believe it lends structure, depth, and just enough earthiness to make any cocktail intriguing and dynamic." Here, it serves as the base for what Leanne envisions as a martini–margarita hybrid. The smoky undercurrent meets tart verjus (pressed juice from unripe wine grapes) and Lustau's fragrant rosé vermouth "for that pop of brightness, conveying the acidity of a margarita," she says. The additions of rhubarb liqueur and Cointreau give the drink texture, a fruity note, and a pink hue. Just a little kiss (besito) of everything we love.

HOW TO MAKE THE DRINK

Add all the ingredients to a mixing glass filled with ice. Stir until cold and strain into a chilled Nick & Nora glass. Express the orange twist over the drink and place it in the glass. Garnish with the orchid, if using, and serve.

DEALER'S
CHOICE

Bring back the '90s!
We'd like an appletini
that's super dry. A
real martini though.
No juice!

SNAP APPLE POP

This is a far cry from the neon green apple martinis of yore. This grown-up version from Miranda Breedlove ticks all the boxes that those never could: It's gin-forward, crisp, tastes like *real* (imagine!) apples, and is awesomely puckery (no, not Pucker!) by way of a green apple shrub she makes herself. "Freezer martinis for the win!" says Breedlove. "Scale the recipe for however many drinks you would like to make, add all the ingredients together, with about ¾ ounce (22.5 ml) of water per drink for dilution, pour it into a bottle, and store in the freezer." Just be sure to garnish each glass with an expressed lemon twist when serving. A tip: While incredibly simple to make, this shrub takes about four days until it's ready to use, so plan accordingly.

CREATOR

**MIRANDA
BREEDLOVE**
Speed Rack competitor

2 ounces (60 ml) Apple-
Infused Gin (recipe follows)

½ ounce (15 ml) dry
vermouth, preferably
Carpano

½ ounce (15 ml) fino sherry,
preferably Lustau

¼ ounce (7.5 ml) Green
Apple Shrub (recipe
follows)

2 dashes Regan's orange
bitters

Lemon twist, for garnish

HOW TO MAKE THE DRINK

Add all the ingredients to a mixing glass filled with ice. Stir until cold and strain into a chilled cocktail glass. Express the lemon twist over the drink and place it in the glass. Serve.

Apple-Infused Gin

*Makes about 25 ounces
(750 ml)*

1 Fuji or Gala apple,
chopped

1 (750-ml) bottle gin,
preferably Beefeater

Combine the chopped apple and gin in an airtight container and let sit at room temperature for 48 hours. Fine strain and pour through a funnel back into the original gin bottle. Store in the refrigerator indefinitely.

Green Apple Shrub

*Makes about 1½ cups
(360 ml)*

3 medium Granny Smith
apples

1 cup (240 ml) apple cider
vinegar

⅔ cup (135 g) granulated
sugar

Shred the apples with a box grater and place in an airtight container. Add the vinegar and sugar and stir until fully integrated. Cover and refrigerate for 4 days. Fine strain and store in an airtight container in the refrigerator for up to 1 month.

DEALER'S CHOICE

—

Give us a maritime martini inspired by the coastal Pacific Northwest.

CREATOR

SIENNA HEMBROOKE-MANN

Speed Rack competitor

¼ ounce (7.5 ml) Salers aperitif

¼ ounce (7.5 ml) gin, preferably Big Gin

¾ ounce (22.5 ml) espadín mezcal, preferably Agave de Cortés Joven

1½ ounces (45 ml) blanc vermouth, preferably La Quintinye Blanc Royal

Cocktail onion, olive, or lemon twist, for garnish

SALERS DELIGHT

For this Dealer's Choice drink, Seattle-based Sienna Hembrooke-Mann didn't have to look far for inspiration. "When walking outside at the end of a shift," she says, "I will often proclaim that the crisp briny air really makes me want a martini!" This is her "maritime martini inspired by those pink skies at night." To bring a sense of freshness, Sienna knew she wanted to pair Salers, a gentian-based clear bitter aperitif with an espadín mezcal from Oaxaca, and a smidge of a juniper-emphatic gin from Seattle. For the vermouth component, "I ended up choosing La Quintinye Blanc for the way it added a silky-smooth mouthfeel that didn't dry the drink out," she says. She says that if you like a drier, more herbaceous martini, it will absolutely work to use a dry vermouth, instead. When it comes to garnishing the Salers Delight, Sienna gives the drinker carte blanche, saying, "It is delicious with no garnish, pickled onion, olives, or a lemon twist." Or why not all three?

HOW TO MAKE THE DRINK

Add all the ingredients to a mixing glass filled with ice. Stir until cold and strain into a chilled Nick & Nora glass. Garnish with a cocktail onion, an olive, a lemon twist—dealer's choice. Serve.

Dear Irving's Gibson (page 201)

Gibson

SPEED RACK • SPINS • THE CLASSICS

Odds are anyone who loves the savory side of a dirty martini will find a friend in the Gibson. Traditionally a 2 parts gin to 1 part vermouth martini, the Gibson features a tart pickled cocktail onion instead of an olive or twist. There are plenty of little companies putting their own spin on these very cute little alliums, but our favorite bartenders make their own—and the effort takes this drink to a new level. We have three distinct versions of the Gibson that make apparent the adaptability of this classic, even with subtle changes, be it swapping bianco vermouth in for dry, tasting the rainbow of cocktail onions, or incorporating sake and fino sherry, as in the Kobayashi Martini on page 180.

THE CLASSIC

GIBSON

2 ounces (60 ml) gin

1 ounce (30 ml) dry vermouth

Cocktail onion, for garnish

Add the gin and vermouth to a mixing glass filled with ice. Stir until cold and strain into a chilled coupe. Garnish with the cocktail onion and serve.

Dear Irving's Gibson

CREATOR
MEAGHAN DORMAN, *Speed Rack judge*

Bianco vermouth is significantly sweeter than the dry vermouth that is traditionally used in a Gibson, playing into the sweetness of the onion. That one change makes this a whole new (but equally delicious) concoction.

2 ounces (60 ml) gin, preferably Tanqueray 10

1 ounce (30 ml) bianco vermouth, preferably Carpano

2 barspoons Onion Brine (recipe follows)

Pickled Onion, for garnish (recipe follows)

Add the gin, vermouth, and onion brine to a mixing glass over ice and stir until cold. Strain into a chilled coupe and garnish with the pickled onion.

PICKLED ONIONS AND BRINE

Makes 20 to 25 onions

2 cups (480 ml) Champagne vinegar

1 cup (200 g) granulated sugar

1 tablespoon salt

½ tablespoon pickling spice (such as McCormick)

8 ounces red pearl onions (about 20 to 25)

Combine the vinegar, sugar, salt, and pickling spice with 1¾ cups (420 ml) water in a saucepan and bring to a boil. Add the onions and boil for 1 minute, then remove from the heat and strain the onions into an airtight container. Store the brine in its own airtight container in the refrigerator for up to 1 month.

Gowanus Gibson

CREATOR
ABIGAIL GULLO, *Speed Rack competitor*

Abigail Gullo has a history with the Gibson: "It was the first drink I tried to order in a 'cocktail bar' when I turned twenty-one," she says. "But I misspoke and ordered a Gimlet instead, so imagine my surprise when I got a mouthful of Rose's lime juice." Eventually, she came to know the cocktail well and made her own adaptation while bartending at Red Hook, Brooklyn's Fort Defiance. The point of pride with this drink is her outrageously pink rainbow onion pickles. "To me, a Gibson is all about the onions, and getting a bit of that good onion juice in the drink," Abigail told us. "Because I use sweet vermouth in the pickling liquid, it gives a rosy tint to the Gibson, and since I created it in Red Hook, I called it the Gowanus Gibson," in honor of the beloved scenic Superfund site, the Gowanus canal.

- 2 ounces (60 ml) gin
- 1 ounce (30 ml) dry vermouth
- 2 dashes orange bitters
- 1 or 2 teaspoons Rainbow Onion Pickle Brine (recipe follows)
- 1 Rainbow Onion Pickle, for garnish (recipe follows)

Add all the ingredients to a mixing glass over ice and stir until cold. Strain into a chilled cocktail glass and garnish with the pickled onion.

RAINBOW ONION PICKLE

Makes 24 pickled onions

- 24 pearl onions (about 8 ounces/225 g), a mix of red, white, and yellow, if possible, root ends trimmed
- ½ cup (120 ml) apple cider (or red wine) vinegar
- 1 tablespoon granulated sugar
- 1½ tablespoons mustard seeds
- ½ teaspoon coriander seeds
- ½ teaspoon rainbow peppercorns
- ½ cup (120 ml) sweet vermouth, something herby and lush such as Carpano Antica or Lustau Vermut
- ¼ cup (60 ml) fino or manzanilla sherry
- 2 sprigs rosemary
- 5 sprigs thyme
- 1 lemon wedge

Bring a large pot of salted water to a boil. Add the onions and cook until just tender, no more than 8 minutes. Drain, rinse under cold water, and drain again. Transfer the onions to a large airtight container.

Meanwhile, in a medium saucepan, combine the vinegar, sugar, mustard seeds, coriander seeds, peppercorns, and ½ cup (120 ml) water and bring to a boil. Cook until the sugar is fully dissolved, about 2 minutes. Remove from the heat and pour the liquid over the onions. Add the sweet vermouth, sherry, rosemary, thyme, and lemon wedge and refrigerate. Your pickles will be ready to go in a few hours, but they get tastier as they sit in the liquid. Store in the refrigerator for up to 2 weeks.

FROM LEFT TO RIGHT, TOP TO BOTTOM: Karla Castaneda takes a second before her round in Season 11 Midwest; judge Bridget Albert asks for a Navy Grog in the same event; Katie Auth kept her free-pouring cool in NYC in Season 11; NOLA showed up for the Redemption competition in Season 10; Carina Soto Velásquez and Monica Berg served as judges in NOLA; Jess Simmons brought Twin City love to Chicago in Season 11; in Season 11, supporters from Maryland, D.C., and Virginia came to NYC in droves.

Eryn Reece stirs up a
Nighthawks (page 208).

GIVE IT TO ME STRAIGHT

DARK, STIRRED, AND BOOZY DRINKS FOR THE BOLD

This book—and Speed Rack itself—is built on classic drinks, but this chapter in particular is home to the actual OG cocktails; all stirred, all boozy, all endlessly riffed upon over the past one hundred fifty or so years.

The benchmark here is the old-fashioned. Pinpointing the precise year and locale of its creation is impossible (it was a style of drink adopted by several bartenders around the same time), but we know from our friend the great cocktail historian Dave Wondrich that the idea of the old-fashioned dates at least as far back as the 1880s. And there's a reason it's endured: It's a reliably and wonderfully simple construct of spirit, sugar, bitters, stirred and served on the rocks.

Around the same time (again, the details are hazy; read Dave's book *Imbibe!*), vermouth became more widely available, and New York City's slightly more complex Manhattan cocktail came along, a 2:1 combination of whiskey and sweet vermouth with a couple of dashes of bitters, stirred and served up.

To this conversation, we'll add something of an outlier, the Negroni, a cocktail that was created just before Prohibition, but one that's only caught on in the American bar scene (and oh, has it ever caught on!) over the past decade. It's based on gin and adds bittersweet Campari to the mix, in a 1:1:1 ratio (gin:Campari:sweet vermouth).

This trio share a commonality in their DNA: They are spirit-led, with subtle sweetness and varying levels of bitterness. Whereas a sour achieves balance via acid (usually citrus) and sugar, these drinks find that harmony via bitters and sugar.

We'd argue that these three are some of the easiest in the Dealer's Choice round. Sure, you can play Potato Head (see page 250) with any classic cocktail equation, but this category of dark or bitter, strong stirred drinks really lends itself to mixing and matching, with massive impact found in one-to-one substitutions.

In their essence, these are drinks that you can make easily, with a quick stop at the liquor store—you don't even need fresh citrus! All the flavors you'll need can come from something you can buy in a bottle.

Many, many classic drinks have been built on the shoulders of these templates. An old-fashioned made with extra bitters and absinthe is a Sazerac (page 254). Made with maraschino and added orange bitters it's a Fancy Free (page 254). Swap scotch for bourbon in a Manhattan and you've made yourself a Rob Roy (page 257), or introduce maraschino to a Manhattan and voila! A Red Hook. The Boulevardier (page 254) is a bourbon take on a Negroni and an Old Pal is just a rye Boulevardier made with dry vermouth.

On the sweet and boozy end of this spectrum, both old-fashioneds and Manhattans are traditionally made with whiskey, but over the years, we've seen them made with everything from aged rum to mezcal. This template gives us the opportunity to consider *any* spirit that has spent some time in wood. So yes, all sorts of whiskey (bourbon, rye, scotch), but also brandies, reposado tequila, aged rum, and on. The char on the inside of the barrels gives these spirits a caramelized note and some extra depth, gravitas.

Split the Difference

These are also good templates for splitting bases, a method that combines spirits, rather than relying on one to carry all the weight, bringing added complexity to cocktails. Though it's certainly not a new idea, it's a move that has become a favorite of bartenders over the last decade. Lynnette says her eyes were first opened to blending base spirits when studying tropical cocktails and delving into the Beachbum Berry philosophy of "what one rum can't do two rums can." Expanding on this to marry spirits makes it possible to amp up (or introduce new) qualities in a drink. Each spirit will contribute its own flavor. An old-fashioned (page 254) becomes infinitely more interesting with a split base, as in the American Trilogy (page 254), which combines rye whiskey with applejack. Kitty Corbo's spin on the Sazerac (page 254) weds rye and Trinidadian rum.

This can go beyond the base spirit. You might also want to try splitting modifiers, such as fortified wines, too. On the sweet vermouth front, some bars now make their own house blends of sweet vermouths (slightly bitter Punt e Mes with the softer French red vermouth Dolin Rouge, say), in order to dial in the flavors they're looking for. The same is true of red aperitivi in Negronis. You can split the Campari with another amaro and find more depth and spice in doing so.

Old-Fashioneds: Sugar and Spice

———•———

Whereas an old-fashioned was historically made with a sugar cube, modern convention has made room for syrups of all sorts—from maple and cane syrup to the plethora of bottled ones from companies like Liber and Small Hand Foods. Or if you're up for it, a tropical old-fashioned is as easy as starting with an aged rum or reposado tequila base, making a pineapple or passion fruit syrup, and adding some island spice bitters. If you're going the way of a Oaxaca Old-Fashioned (page 257), use agave nectar to align with the tequila and mezcal in the base. And remember! As with any stirred drink, the trick with the old-fashioneds is dialing in the dilution—getting the drink cold without it being watery—we recommend investing in some nice silicone ice cube trays (see Resources, page 259), especially if you want a big, beautiful rock.

Manhattans: Not Just for Vermouth Anymore

———•———

On the Manhattan front, its identity as a drink made with sweet vermouth has evolved, too. Vermouth is essentially wine with sugar and a whole bunch of botanicals, which bring varying levels of bitterness and herbal qualities. Knowing this brings a whole spectrum of ingredients, including other fortified wines, sherries (especially barrel-aged ones like amontillado and oloroso as well as sweet cream sherry), amari, green and yellow Chartreuse, and quinquinas into the Manhattan conversation. New York City has long been known as a place where drinks were bitter, brown, and stirred, and over the years numerous riffs on the Manhattan have been made in tribute to other city neighborhoods and boroughs. The Brooklyn is an old standby, but in the last twenty years, Red Hook, Greenpoint, and Bensonhurst have all gotten their own, utilizing various modifiers along the way. Ivy's Perfect BQE (page 210) unites several of these parts of town with dry and sweet vermouths, green Chartreuse, and a touch of maraschino.

Negronis: The Ultimate Flex

———•———

So, too, there are infinite ways to plug and play with the Negroni's equal parts recipe. The White Negroni, made with Suze, bianco vermouth, and gin, is a brilliant modern classic that shows the flexibility of the drink. But it can go to the dark side, too, with aged tequila and rum. In the same way that the Manhattan swaps other modifiers for sweet vermouth, so too can the Negroni. And while Campari is the gold standard, it is by no means the only bitter liqueur that will work here. Try a lighter sweeter take with Aperol or Contratto Bitter, which is slightly less bitter than Campari. There are several American-made red aperitivi out there now too, including a lighter one from Forthave Spirits in New York and another, the nicely spiced Bruto Americano from St. George Spirits in California. All are worth experimenting with.

As with martinis, both Manhattans and old-fashioneds are smart places to accentuate flavors in the base spirit with bitters. It's very easy to go crazy amassing tons of these tiny bottles, but it's fun to have a few options outside the standard Angostura, Peychaud's, and orange. Dash in an extra layer of "what *is* that?!" with flavors like eucalyptus! Mole! Habanero! You won't need to add bitters to drinks that are made with intensely bitter amaros.

From a stepped-up Rob Roy from Rob Roy queen Anu Apte, to a take-on-a-throwback brandy cocktail from Zulcoralis Rodríguez, the pages that follow have everything you need to stir up a dark, bitter, and mysterious evening.

NIGHTHAWKS

CREATOR

ERYN REECE
Speed Rack competitor,
USA national winner

1½ ounces (45 ml) mezcal,
preferably Del Maguey Vida

¾ ounce (22.5 ml)
amontillado sherry,
preferably Lustau

½ ounce (15 ml) sweet
vermouth, preferably
Carpano Antica

½ ounce (15 ml) coffee
liqueur, preferably Caffe
Lolita

¼ ounce (7.5 ml) Ancho
Reyes Original

1 dash Bittermens Xocolatl
mole bitters

Named for the iconic late-night Edward Hopper painting, Eryn Reece's Nighthawks cocktail (photo on page 204) is at its core a mezcal Manhattan, but with layers of spice, coffee, and sherry notes that take the drink to an intriguingly brooding place. Eryn was a fundamental part of Speed Rack's creation and is an important member of the family. The first time Lynnette met Eryn—back in 2009—she was working at Louis 649, a bar in New York City's East Village. "I was like 'who's this woman!?'" says Lynnette. It was this happy meeting that inspired Lynnette to establish a New York City branch of LUPEC (Ladies United for the Preservation of Endangered Cocktails) that was in many ways a jumping-off point for Speed Rack itself. Lynnette wanted to find a way to bring together all of the badass women who were quietly doing the hard work behind bars around the city. Not only was Eryn a founding member of LUPEC, but she was Speed Rack's national champion in Season 2 and she's been one of our most dedicated mentors ever since.

HOW TO MAKE THE DRINK

Add all the ingredients to a mixing glass filled with ice. Stir until cold and strain into a chilled Nick & Nora glass. Serve.

DEALER'S
CHOICE

———

Can you make us a
fruity dark and boozy
cocktail?

CREATOR

IRENE KERN
Speed Rack competitor

———

1 dash Angostura bitters

1 dash orange bitters,
preferably Regan's

1 ounce (30 ml) rye whiskey,
preferably Rittenhouse

1 ounce (30 ml) Calvados,
preferably Calvados du
Pays D'Auge

¾ ounce (22.5 ml) Brucato
Woodlands Amaro

Maraschino cherry on a
pick and a lemon twist, for
garnish

SWEATER WEATHER

"Whenever I hear 'Manhattan,' my brain immediately thinks spirit-forward and boozy. I really loved working with a prompt that let me create a cocktail that was simultaneously stirred and spirit-driven, as well as layered and fruity," says Irene Kern, who is a bartender in San Francisco. Here, we have a split-base Manhattan that holds onto the usual rye whiskey, but brings on some fruity complexity with Calvados, an apple brandy made in France's Normandy region. Calvados is aged a minimum of two years in oak, which gives it depth and structure similar to that of the rye. Feel free to play with other aged apple brandies, or even applejack (which is made from apples, boosted with neutral grain spirit), knowing that they will vary in age and texture. Irene replaces the drink's usual sweet vermouth with a hometown favorite amaro from Brucato, which is made in San Francisco. "Their Woodlands expression stands up well to the strong personalities of the rye and Calvados; the fig and chocolate notes in the amaro bringing an intriguing depth and richness," she says. This drink (photo on page 211) is boosted with a couple dashes of bitters, which Irene recommends putting in the mixing glass first, as it can be easy to forget them at the end. Speed Rack competitors, take note.

HOW TO MAKE THE DRINK

Add all the ingredients to a mixing glass filled with ice. Stir until cold and strain into a chilled Nick & Nora glass. Express the lemon twist over the glass and discard. Garnish with the cherry on a pick. Serve.

CREATOR

IVY MIX
Speed Rack co-founder

2 ounces (60 ml) rye whiskey, preferably Wild Turkey 101

½ ounce (15 ml) dry vermouth, preferably Dolin

½ ounce (15 ml) sweet vermouth, preferably Cocchi di Torino

¼ ounce (7.5 ml) green Chartreuse

1 teaspoon maraschino liqueur

Maraschino cherry, for garnish

PERFECT BQE

For this drink, I wanted to combine two of my favorite Manhattan riffs—the Red Hook (itself a Brooklyn-Manhattan mashup made with rye, Punt e Mes, and maraschino liqueur) and the Greenpoint (rye with sweet vermouth and yellow Chartreuse), both of which were created by bartenders at New York's legendary Milk & Honey bar. I love splitting my bases and do it all the time, but it took me a bit of messing around to realize that this cocktail is best as a *perfect* Manhattan. Drinks are described as "perfect" when made with a split of sweet and dry vermouth; it's a technique that comes in handy when you need to balance out sweetness, as I did here with the Chartreuse and maraschino. The name for the cocktail is itself very Brooklyn insider: I thought about what actually connects the two Brooklyn neighborhoods of Red Hook and Greenpoint and the answer is the Brooklyn-Queens Expressway, aka the BQE.

HOW TO MAKE THE DRINK

Add all the ingredients to a mixing glass filled with ice. Stir until cold and strain into a chilled Nick & Nora glass. Garnish with the maraschino cherry and serve.

Perfect BQE (page 210), Sweater Weather (page 209)

Can you give us a
split whiskey-base
riff on a Rob Roy?

CREATOR

ANU APTE
*Speed Rack competitor
and judge*

1½ ounces (45 ml) blended
scotch, preferably The
Feathery

½ ounce (15 ml) single-malt
scotch, preferably Tamdhu

1 ounce (30 ml) sweet
vermouth, preferably Dolin
Rouge

3 dashes apple bitters

Groomed lemon twist, for
garnish (see headnote)

ELEGANT ROB ROY

Anu Apte is the reigning queen of the Seattle cocktail scene. She opened her bar, Rob Roy, in 2009 and it remains one of the best places to get a drink on the West Coast, with an intense devotion to the classics. Clearly, we had to ask her for a variation on the Rob Roy (page 257), a drink that dates to the mid 1900s and, which, itself, is a variation on a Manhattan, where scotch is subbed for bourbon or rye. Here, Anu uses two scotches: one blended, The Feathery, and one single malt, Tamdhu, both aged in ex-oloroso sherry barrels. "I want to keep it elegant, so I was careful to not use a robust single malt scotch that is smoky or peaty," she says. "Of course, make sure you pour your drink into a *chilled* coupe or rocks glass, and don't forget to pack the ice up to about 3 inches from the top of the mixing glass," Anu advises. After using a citrus peeler to make her lemon twist, Anu uses a sharp knife to cut around the edges to give the twist a nice, clean-cut appearance—a groomed lemon twist.

HOW TO MAKE THE DRINK

Chill a mixing glass and a coupe or rocks glass. Add all the ingredients to a mixing glass filled with ice. Stir for 10 to 12 seconds, taking care not to over-dilute. Strain into a chilled coupe or rocks glass. Express the lemon twist over the drink, place it in the glass, and serve.

CREATOR

**ALISHA
NEVERSON**
Speed Rack competitor

1 dash Angostura bitters

1 dash cardamom bitters

½ ounce (15 ml) cassis,
preferably Current Cassis

½ ounce (15 ml) Cappelletti
Amaro Sfumato Rabarbaro

2 ounces (60 ml) cognac

Maraschino cherry,
preferably Luxardo, for
garnish

UNDER THE VEIL

We love a take on a take. This, from Alisha Neverson, is her variation on a Black Manhattan, which adheres to the standard 2:1 Manhattan formula, simply swapping the vermouth with bitter Averna, a dark and brooding amaro. Alisha sticks to using a barrel-aged spirit as the base here, but rather than whiskey, she uses cognac, which has a "similar bitter and spiced profile, yet offers a broader range of fruit and floral, as well," she says. Rather than using just amaro, Alisha splits cassis and Cappelletti's Sfumato Rabarbaro, an intensely smoky amaro for added layers, finishing with Angostura and cardamom bitters to further accentuate the aroma of the drink. She offers this advice when it comes to stirring drinks that will be served up: "I've learned to crack in a few cubes while filling your stirring glass with whole cubes for better chill and dilution."

HOW TO MAKE THE DRINK

Add all the ingredients to a mixing glass and then start to layer in ice, with whole cubes to cover the bottom, a couple of cracked cubes on top, and then more cubes to fill the glass. Stir until cold and strain into a chilled cocktail glass. Garnish with the cherry and serve.

DEALER'S
CHOICE

Make us your best
Parisian cocktail. A
Manhattan riff but
French and on the
rocks.

CREATOR

**BRITTINI RAE
PETERSON**
*Speed Rack competitor,
USA national winner*

1¾ ounces (55.5 ml)
Cognac, preferably Martell
Swift

¾ ounce (22.5 ml) Punt
e Mes

½ ounce (15 ml) maple
syrup

2 dashes peach bitters

2 dashes Peychaud's bitters

An orange twist and a
lemon twist, for garnish

PLACE DE LA CONCORDE

"I imagine people sipping this in the Hôtel de Crillon or Hôtel de la Marine looking out onto the Place de la Concorde in the heart of Paris," says Brittini Rae Peterson of her take on a cognac-based Manhattan-meets-old-fashioned. Here, bitter Punt e Mes serves as the sweet vermouth and a touch of maple syrup rounds out any sharp edges. "Be careful not to overstir," she says. "Part of the joy of this cocktail is how the flavor expands over time in the glass." The drink will gradually change as the ice melts. Whereas most bartenders are a little obsessive about ice, Brittini Rae has taken this to a whole new level as the owner of the Nice Company in Paris, which creates stunning, crystal-clear cubes, spheres, and beyond, for bars. "If you have clear ice, make sure you take it out of your freezer five minutes before to allow it to temper. Ice that is too cold can dampen flavors," she says. Brittini pours her Place de la Concorde over a large perfectly hewn cube, *bien sûr!*

HOW TO MAKE THE DRINK

Add all the ingredients to a mixing glass filled with ice. Stir until cold and strain into a chilled rocks glass over a large ice cube. Express the citrus twists over the drink and place them in the glass. Serve.

CREATOR

RHACHEL SHAW
Speed Rack competitor

¾ ounce (22.5 ml) overproof rye, preferably Old Overholt Bonded Overproof Rye

¾ ounce (22.5 ml) applejack, preferably Laird's Straight Apple Brandy—Bottled in Bond

½ ounce (15 ml) palo cortado sherry

½ ounce (15 ml) Tempus Fugit Crème de Banane

3 dashes Peychaud's bitters

Lemon twist, for garnish

VIEUX POMPIER

Without Rhachel Shaw, Speed Rack simply wouldn't exist. "I was on the boat in the bay where it all started," she says. It's true. The day that Speed Rack was first dreamed up, Ivy and Rhachel were floating around the San Francisco Bay with a few fellow bartenders talking about how female bartenders weren't taken seriously. They joked around about doing a video series they would call "Speed Rack" to highlight the tokenism of why most women they knew were asked to work events: not because of who they were but, essentially, because they had breasts. After that fateful day, Ivy went to Lynnette with the name Speed Rack and the desire to do something to promote and support the women+ folk within the cocktail community. In surprisingly short measure, Rhachel found herself competing in the first season— and has helped us out with events in San Francisco and Los Angeles ever since. "I do love a strong drink, but I also wanted a balanced drink," she says about her take on the Vieux Carré, a New Orleans standby. "I tried to stick to the classic specs but the ingredients I wanted to use weren't working in that way." She'd set out to use Old Overholt Overproof Rye, which is quite assertive, so the rest of her ingredients had to accommodate the base. Here, sweet palo cortado sherry stands in for the vermouth and banana liqueur for the herbal liqueur—a softer, gentler, and perhaps tropical take on a Big Easy favorite.

HOW TO MAKE THE DRINK

Add all the ingredients to a mixing glass filled with ice and stir until cold. Strain into a chilled rocks glass. Express the lemon twist over the drink, place it in the glass, and serve.

CREATOR

ZULCORALIS "ZULCO" RODRÍGUEZ
Speed Rack competitor, regional winner

---

2 ounces (60 ml) brandy, preferably Seven Tails XO

¾ ounce (22.5 ml) white port, preferably Warre's

2 teaspoons Nonino L'Aperitivo

1 teaspoon turbinado sugar

Grapefruit twist, for garnish

LEGIONNAIRE

We love it when a competitor whips out a vintage cocktail that no one ever thinks of in the Dealer's Choice round. Here, Zulco Rodríguez, an incredibly focused, well-studied bartender, originally from Puerto Rico but currently ruling the roost in Houston, took the assignment for a brandy cocktail and made her version of a brandy sangaree. "I wanted to create a spirituous but subtle cocktail, as a late-night sipper," she told us. Sangarees harken back to the late eighteenth century, often made from wine or brandy mixed with sugar, water, and spices. It's assumed to be the predecessor to sangria. Brandy is often underrepresented on cocktail lists, which is kind of surprising given how vast the category is. It encompasses spirits distilled from fruit and includes everything from Calvados to cognac to Spanish brandy to eaux de vie. Here, Zulco combines three grape-based ingredients: a French brandy, white port, and Nonino's L'Aperitivo—the latter two bringing their own spice notes. After competing in five seasons of Speed Rack, Zulco is now one of our most diligent mentors in Texas. "Speed Rack has given me resources, opportunities, and exposure that not only helps me to constantly improve myself, but it allows me to serve as an inspiration for the industry as well," she says.

HOW TO MAKE THE DRINK

Add all the ingredients to a mixing glass and stir to fully dissolve the sugar. Fill the glass with ice and stir until cold. Strain into a rocks glass over 1 large ice cube. Express the grapefruit twist over the drink, discard, and serve.

Negroni

CLOCKWISE
FROM TOP LEFT:
Psycho Killer
(page 224),
Hibiscus No-Groni
(page 223),
A.O.C. (page 224)

SPEED RACK
SPINS
THE
CLASSICS

Over the past decade, the Negroni, 1:1:1 gin : sweet vermouth : Campari, has become one of the most frequently ordered drinks around the country. It's as if everyone decided all at once that bitter things might be kind of good. We are completely here for this nationwide obsession. The following are three variations on the Negroni that give us a deeper understanding of the potential of this seemingly simple stirred drink.

NEGRONI

1 ounce (30 ml) gin

1 ounce (30 ml) Campari

1 ounce (30 ml) sweet vermouth

Orange twist, for garnish

Add all the ingredients to a mixing glass over ice. Stir until chilled and strain into a rocks glass over ice or strain into a chilled coupe. Express the orange twist over the drink, place in the glass, and serve.

CACAO-INFUSED CAMPARI

Makes about 1 cup (240 ml)

1 cup (240 ml) Campari

1 tablespoon cacao nibs

Add the Campari and cacao nibs to a lidded jar. Cap the jar and shake to combine, then let the mixture infuse for 1 hour at room temperature, shaking it every so often. Strain into an airtight container and store in the fridge for up to 1 month.

Hibiscus No-Groni

CREATOR

LEANNE FAVRE, *Speed Rack competitor*

With the popularity of the Negroni, and the sonic boom in non-alcoholic cocktails, bars everywhere have been trying their best to engineer a zero-proof Negroni. This, created by Leanne Favre for Ivy's Brooklyn bar, Leyenda, masterfully gets at the sweet, bitter, citrusy notes found in Campari, thanks to a hibiscus bitter that she makes using ingredients typical of red bitter aperitivi: hibiscus, gentian root, and orange. This is used in combination with Seedlip's no-alc Grove for its "hints of citrus and a touch of ginger spice that plays well with tropical bitter hibiscus and adds depth to the cocktail."

1½ ounces (45 ml) Hibiscus Bitter (recipe follows)

1½ ounces (45 ml) Seedlip Grove 42 distilled non-alcoholic spirit

Orange twist and hibiscus leaf, for garnish

Add all the ingredients to a rocks glass over 1 big ice cube. Express the orange twist over the drink and place it in the glass. Garnish with the hibiscus leaf, and serve.

HIBISCUS BITTER

Makes about 3 cups (240 ml)

3 tablespoons dried hibiscus flowers (see Resources, page 259)

1 tablespoon dried gentian root (see Resources, page 259)

1 tablespoon dried orange peel

1¼ cups (250 g) granulated sugar

Combine all the ingredients, except the sugar, with 2½ cups (600 ml) water in a saucepan and bring to a boil over medium heat. Remove from the heat and let steep for 30 minutes. Strain into an airtight container and whisk in the sugar until fully dissolved. Cover and store in the refrigerator for up to 1 week.

A.O.C.

CREATOR
LYNNETTE MARRERO, *Speed Rack co-founder*

For a Speed Rack Women's History Month event in 2019, Haley Traub (see page 248) and I made cocktails inspired by groundbreaking women in politics. I made the A.O.C. (with Altos tequila, oloroso sherry, and Campari) to complement Haley's Ruth Bader "Gin"sburg. I replaced the gin with tequila and the traditional Italian vermouth with Spanish sherry. And by infusing the Campari with cacao, I can bridge the nuttiness of the sherry with the sweeter spice notes in the reposado tequila.

1½ ounces (45 ml) reposado tequila, preferably Altos

1 ounce (30 ml) oloroso sherry, preferably Lustau

1 ounce (30 ml) Cacao-Infused Campari (recipe follows)

Grapefruit twist, for garnish

Add all the ingredients to a mixing glass over ice. Stir until chilled and strain into a rocks glass over ice. Express the grapefruit twist over the drink, place it in the glass, and serve.

Psycho Killer

CREATOR
JILLIAN VOSE, *Speed Rack competitor*

"I was mapping out a massive cocktail menu and one must have some kind of Negroni or Boulevardier variation. It dawned on me that there wasn't a known classic Irish whiskey variation and so I set out to make one," says Jillian Vose. Campari is big, very sweet, and very bitter, which necessitated a substantial whiskey; Jillian chose Redbreast 12-year Single Pot Still. "The rich Christmas cake and dried fruit notes I was getting from it, it seemed pretty obvious to me that banana and chocolate were good bets." She swapped the vermouth for a blend of liqueurs and a tiny dose of absinthe for a drink that is robust and warming through and through.

2 ounces (60 ml) Irish whiskey, preferably Redbreast 12-year Single Pot Still

¾ ounce (22.5 ml) Campari

½ ounce (15 ml) Giffard Banane du Brésil liqueur

½ ounce (15 ml) Giffard Crème de Cacao

1 dash absinthe, preferably Vieux Pontarlier

Add all the ingredients to a mixing glass filled with ice. Stir until cold and strain into a Nick & Nora glass. Serve.

CREATOR

KITTY CORBO
*Speed Rack competitor,
USA national winner*

¼ ounce (7.5 ml) Herbsaint
anise-flavored liqueur

1 ounce (30 ml) rye whiskey,
preferably Sazerac

1 ounce (30 ml) Jung &
Wulff Trinidad rum

½ ounce (15 ml) pineapple
syrup (see Resources,
page 259)

4 to 5 dashes Peychaud's
bitters

Lemon twist, for garnish

CARACARA

The Sazerac (page 254), a concoction of anise-y Herbsaint, rye whiskey, simple syrup, and Peychaud's bitters, is arguably the best-known drink to come out of New Orleans. Looking to preserve what she calls "the heart of the Sazerac," Kitty Corbo searched for another spirit that would complement the spiciness of the rye and the herbal notes from the Herbsaint. "I did a split-based aged rum cocktail in my final Dealer's Choice round in 2019, so I thought it would be appropriate to bring rum into this creation," she says. Here, she's pulled in a Trinidadian rum from Jung & Wulff. And to give her Sazerac more of a tropical vibe, Kitty uses a sweet pineapple syrup to welcome the nuances of the aged rum to the party.

HOW TO MAKE THE DRINK

Rinse a rocks glass with the Herbsaint, discard any excess, and set the glass aside. Add the rye, rum, pineapple syrup, and bitters to a mixing glass filled with ice. Stir until cold and strain into the prepared rocks glass. Express the lemon twist over the drink and place it in the glass. Serve.

Low-Lying Clouds (page 229)

CHAPTER
8

DRINK YOUR DESSERT

DECADENT DRINKS, DIGESTIFS, AND NIGHTCAPS

What do you order when you've just finished dinner, but you're not quite ready to call the evening quits? Between the two of us, we have very different takes. For Ivy, it's all about drinking her dessert—the richer and creamier, the better. Bring on the Brandy Alexanders, egg-fortified flips, and cozy hot toddies! Whereas Lynnette prefers to end her day maybe with a little sherry or amaro—nothing too decadent. She'd go for a reverse Manhattan, heavy on the vermouth, or maybe a darker mezcal drink, like Eryn Reece's Nighthawks (page 208), a little sweetness but with a little heat, too.

In this chapter, we're serving up examples that run that gamut from sweet and luxurious to what you might call "soft landings." Whatever the Dealer's Choices in the nightcap realm, none of these "last drinks" swing too far in that uber sugary, thick, and rich direction; these ladies were deliberate in balancing sweetness with bitterness or smoke or even a little kick of pepper.

Bitter Endings

———•———

Let's consider the after-dinner genre starting with the bitter side of things. If you seek nightcaps with a digestif aspect, this is a great moment for you. We are in the glory days of amaro, those herbal, spiced liqueurs that originated in Italy and are traditionally consumed after a meal. The amaro boom has seen them emerging from around the world, from lightly bitter to intensely dark and bracing, with flavors that vary from orangey to spiced to deeply herbal. They're perfect stand-alone digestifs, neat or over ice, but included in cocktails, their digestif character holds true. Here, Kapri Robinson's Cat's Got Your Tongue (page 237) is a fuller take on a Negroni, with two amari and warming allspice dram. And Jess Yurko's Talking in Cursive (page 244) uses just a touch of Montenegro amaro (a light-in-body but boldly bitter pick) to balance out a whiskey and genever–based take on an old-fashioned.

Soft Landings

———•———

For something in the less boozy vein, incorporating sherry or other fortified wines into a post-prandial drink will naturally scale down its alcohol, a nice move after a long night of imbibing to be sure. Consider using oxidative sherries like olorosos or amontillados to give a slightly richer, toasty note or some PX sherry for a little sweetness. Riffing on a Manhattan, Colie Ehrenworth's Sherry Tale Ending (page 239) blends barrel-aged reposado with amontillado and maple syrup, all with a roasted, caramelized vibe.

Smooth Finishes

———•———

Fat and sugar go very well together and there's a time and a place for something like a frothy, minty Grasshopper or an old-school scotch and gin–based Barbary Coast (page 257), both of which not only call for dairy, but for crème de cacao, a chocolate liqueur that can reinforce that indulgence.

We now have so many dairy alternatives that anyone looking to avoid dairy can still get in on a luscious drink. In her warm cocktail Cuddle Storm (page 236), Ivy makes use of oat milk. And Lynnette splits coconut cream with cashew milk in her piña colada variation, Pineapple Crown (page 139).

Lush flip-style drinks incorporate an entire egg, resulting in cocktails that are the epitome of drinking your dessert. It's basically alcoholic custard! A very old category of cocktail, dating back to early American times, that can utilize any spirit, but the classics use sherry or brandy. The mission with flips is to aerate through vigorous shaking so that they don't feel heavy like a milkshake. To achieve this cloudlike fluffiness, dry shake the cocktail first (that is, without ice) and then add ice and shake again to chill it down. We love Jessi Pollak's applejack-and-amontillado flip that recalls apple pie, the À La Mode (page 243).

The espresso martini (page 258), a modern classic conceived by British bartender all-star Dick Bradsell back in the '80s, has made a serious comeback; you'll feel its influence in several drinks in this chapter. One variation that's near and dear to our hearts is Haley Traub's Matriarch Martini (page 248), a tribute to her nana, a three-time breast cancer survivor. Haley's version is darker and fruitier, with bourbon standing in for the vodka and a little tart cherry juice to brighten things up. We won't blame you if you opt for decaf espresso in the wee hours, but please do raise a glass to all things pink.

Whether you're in Ivy's dessert-in-a-glass camp or Lynnette's anything-but-cream corner, there's for sure something for you to explore in the following pages.

CREATOR

JENA ELLENWOOD
Speed Rack competitor

¼ ounce (7.5 ml) allspice dram

¼ ounce (7.5 ml) Giffard Vanille de Madagascar liqueur

½ ounce (15 ml) crème de cacao, preferably Tempus Fugit

1½ ounces (45 ml) Irish whiskey, preferably J.J. Corry The Hanson

1 ounce (30 ml) coconut cream

Freshly grated dark chocolate and cinnamon, for garnish

LOW-LYING CLOUDS

The traditional Alexander (equal parts spirit, crème de cacao, and cream) is perhaps an unsung hero of the after-dinner drink compendium, but it is undeniably delicious and a genius formula to follow for a modern Irish cream. When she thought about an Irish whiskey dessert cocktail, the aromas of coconut and aging whiskey floated into Jena's mind. Her iteration (photo on page 226), named for a painting by Jane Ramey, an artist based in Northern Ireland, is dairy-free, with coconut cream bringing the richness, and the crème de cacao split with a little bit of warming allspice dram and vanilla liqueur for added complexity. Jena's participation in Speed Rack came not only as a means of challenging herself but also connecting to a cause that deeply resonated with her and her family. "My aunt is a breast cancer survivor, and the day of my competition was the anniversary of my cousin's passing from leukemia. I competed as a tribute to them," she says.

HOW TO MAKE THE DRINK

Add all the ingredients to a shaker filled with ice. Shake until cold and strain into a chilled Nick & Nora glass. Grate the dark chocolate and cinnamon over the top of the drink, and serve.

It's after dinner but
we must go on! Can
you make us a drink to
transition from dinner
to late night?

CREATOR

BAYLEE HOPINGS
*Speed Rack competitor,
regional winner*

¾ ounce (22.5 ml) mezcal,
preferably Bahnez

¾ ounce (22.5 ml) blanco
tequila, preferably
Cimarron

¾ ounce (22.5 ml) oloroso
sherry, preferably
Gonzalez-Byass Alfonso

½ ounce (15 ml) Tempus
Fugit crème de cacao

1 dash Fee Brothers Aztec
Chocolate bitters

Lemon twist, for garnish

SIN NOMBRE

While all Speed Rack competitors come to prelims with a solid grasp of formulas for the classics (and modern classics), some also have secret weapon formulas of their own that they'll put to use when it comes to Dealer's Choice. For Baylee Hopings, when she's creating stirred cocktails, she'll often work from a template of 1 ½ ounces (45 ml) base spirit to ¾ ounce (22.5 ml) fortified wine to ¼ or ½ ounce (7.5 or 15 ml) liqueur, plus bitters. For this after-dinner pick-me-up, she knew that she wanted to use Tempus Fugit's Crème de Cacao, which she plugged in as the liqueur. To complement that, she reached for a nutty oloroso sherry as the fortified wine because nuts and chocolate . . . yes, please. When it came to the base spirit, "I thought it would be nice to have the roasty agave and smoke notes you get from mezcal," Baylee says. To prevent this from overwhelming the other flavors with the drink, she split the base with tequila. And Aztec chocolate bitters brought the whole thing together. "Just be sure you choose a mezcal with at least a moderate level of smoke so that it comes through," she says.

HOW TO MAKE THE DRINK

Add all the ingredients to a mixing glass filled with ice. Stir until cold and strain into a chilled Nick & Nora glass. Express the lemon twist over the drink, place it in the glass, and serve.

Could you make us
your variation on a
traditional Mexican
after-dinner drink?

K ESPRESSO MARTINI

CREATOR

BRISA SANTOS C.
*Speed Rack competitor,
Mexico winner*

2 ounces (60 ml) cold coffee

¾ ounce (22.5 ml) yellow
Chartreuse

1½ ounces (45 ml) vodka

A few coffee beans, for
garnish, if desired

"I decided to compete mostly because I wanted to lose the fear of trying new and challenging things," says Brisa Santos C. "I really believe
in the Speed Rack cause; I wanted to show all women fighting through
something that there are people out there working hard to support them
in any way possible." At twenty-three years old, Brisa blew everyone
away in our final round in Mexico City, a metropolis with a thrilling,
blossoming cocktail scene. Riding this high, here she combined two of
her favorite classic cocktails, the espresso martini (page 258) and the
Last Word (page 255), in this simple and complete coffee drink; it's so
unexpected, intriguingly dry and bitter in the best way.

HOW TO MAKE THE DRINK

Add all the ingredients to a cocktail shaker filled with ice. Shake until
cold and strain into a chilled Nick & Nora glass. Top with a few coffee beans,
if using, and serve.

CLOCKWISE FROM TOP RIGHT:
K Espresso Martini (page 232),
S'more of What (with cookie) (page 234),
Almond Joyful Old-Fashioned (page 235)

We're going camping
and want to pack
a nightcap to drink
around the campfire.
What are you putting
in our thermos?

CREATOR

NATASHA MESA
*Speed Rack competitor,
regional winner*

1 ounce (30 ml) single
malt scotch, preferably
Auchentoshan

½ ounce (15 ml) blended
scotch, preferably Johnnie
Walker Black

1 ounce (30 ml) espresso

½ ounce (15 ml) Averna
amaro

¼ ounce (7.5 ml) Meletti
Cioccolato chocolate
liqueur

¼ ounce (7.5 ml) coffee
liqueur

2 dashes Fee Brothers
Walnut bitters

S'MORE OF WHAT

Natasha Mesa's ability to evoke a moment in time through her cocktails
is strong, as evidenced by this take on an espresso martini (page 258).
"My mind first went to the mornings and nights on the Oregon coast: the
cool breeze, the salinity in the air, and the smell of campfire. Naturally,
I was drawn to scotch with its notes of coconut, salt, and smoke," she
says. As with many spirits, scotch can have such a range of flavors, and
Natasha's very intentional with the two expressions she combines here.
But if you're a scotch lover, take this as an opportunity to experiment.
She notes that odds are if you're *actually* camping, you probably won't
have a cocktail shaker. (Or maybe you will! Priorities!) "Just use a jar
with a lid," she says.

HOW TO MAKE THE DRINK

Add all the ingredients to a cocktail shaker filled with ice. Shake until cold,
double strain into a flask or chilled coupe, and serve.

ALMOND JOYFUL OLD-FASHIONED

CREATOR

LYNNETTE
MARRERO
Speed Rack co-founder

2 ounces (60 ml) aged rum,
preferably Zacapa No. 23

½ ounce (15 ml) coconut
syrup, preferably Liber &
Co.

1 dash Angostura bitters

1 dash almond extract

1 dash high-quality vanilla
extract

Freshly grated nutmeg, for
garnish

Here's a reference to my favorite candy bar as a kid, the Almond Joy. As an adult, I love pairing chocolate and aged rum, and I wanted to explore those flavors. Using a rum that has a sherry finish brings out nuttiness, so I reflected that with the almond, and the coconut syrup takes the place of the sugar. So many of these flavors—coconut, vanilla, and almond—are also characteristics that I love in barrel-aged spirits. This old-fashioned is a decadent treat.

HOW TO MAKE THE DRINK

Add all the ingredients to a double old-fashioned glass over ice. Stir gently. Garnish with nutmeg, and serve.

FROM THE FOUNDERS

—

Make this for yourself!
Drink it while you take
some much-needed
ME time and get cozy
with a book.

CREATOR

IVY MIX
Speed Rack co-founder

1½ ounces (45 ml) bourbon,
preferably Elijah Craig

½ ounce (15 ml) poire
williams pear brandy

1 tablespoon honey

5 ounces (150 ml) oat milk

Freshly grated nutmeg, for
garnish

CUDDLE STORM

As Lynnette can attest, I *love* a creamy drink. We've traveled the world together doing Speed Rack, and whenever there is a creamy drink on a menu, Lynnette just knows and will order me one. That's what a great work wife is all about! Served warm, this drink is one I make for myself when I am home and I just want to feel comforted. Maybe I read a book, maybe I watch a show, but I want a warm liquid hug. Just take care when heating this up. Slow and low is the name of the game. Be sure not to let it boil, as it will burn off the alcohol (and who wants that?) and just taste burnt (gross). And make sure to preheat your mug ahead of time with hot water, so the cold mug doesn't steal the warmth of the drink. In my opinion, this is best consumed when there's snow falling.

HOW TO MAKE THE DRINK

Add all the ingredients to a small saucepan over low heat. Fill a mug with hot water (from the tap is fine), let it sit for a minute or two, and discard the water. When the mixture is hot but not boiling, pour into the warmed mug, garnish with nutmeg, and serve.

DEALER'S CHOICE

What's your perfect silky-smooth drink for treating yourself after a long night?

CREATOR

KAPRI ROBINSON
Speed Rack competitor

1½ ounces (45 ml) gin, preferably Barr Hill Tom Cat

½ ounce (15 ml) Luxardo Amaro Abano

¼ ounce (7.5 ml) Luxardo Bitter Rosso

¼ ounce (7.5 ml) allspice dram

3 dashes Hella Cocktail Co. Eucalyptus bitters

Orange twist, for garnish

CAT'S GOT YOUR TONGUE

Kapri Robinson is on a tear. She says, "Speed Rack has expanded my network to a national gaze!" but we know better than that—people were going to know this woman no matter what. She was a contestant on the Netflix series *Drink Masters* and a finalist for Best US Bartender at Tales of the Cocktail in 2022 and she also started her own cocktail competition, Chocolate City's Best for Black and Brown bartenders in Washington, D.C. She's unstoppable. She tells us this nightcap came to her while celebrating over the holidays. "I created this cocktail on the second night of Kwanzaa and while I lit my candles, I wanted to sit and watch the flame while sipping on a smooth, stirred drink. This cocktail's color came out close to the red of the pan-African flag." Working with her favorite base spirit, gin, Kapri played off a Negroni build, looking to increase the richness and bring out the more herbal characteristics of the drink. Here, she uses not one but two amari to add more layers of complexity that are accentuated by sweet allspice dram and freshening eucalyptus bitters.

HOW TO MAKE THE DRINK

Add all the ingredients to a mixing glass filled with ice. Stir until cold and strain into a rocks glass over 1 large ice cube. Express the orange twist over the drink, place it in the glass, and serve.

Oh Canada! We
would love to end
the evening on a
lighter note—and let's
sweeten the deal with
some maple syrup.

SHERRY TALE ENDING

"I think making stirred cocktails is a fun challenge because you don't have the citrus and sugar to hide behind. You really have to nail down the intent behind the cocktail," says Colie Ehrenworth. Colie, a Toronto-based bartender, competed in Canada's fourth season of Speed Rack in 2019 after being roped in by Tess Anne Sawyer, who won in Canada's Season 2. "I had only been bartending for about six months and she was absolutely right that training for the competition would make me a much more efficient, overall better bartender," she told us. For this drink, Colie's intent was to blend two ingredients that she herself gravitates toward as nightcaps: tequila and sherry. With a nod to a classic Adonis (page 258), which blends fino sherry and sweet vermouth, and building off the Manhattan (page 254) template, she subbed in toasty amontillado, with a little Lillet Blanc and maple sugar syrup for a cocktail that just toes the line of sweet. She advises using real *Ontario* maple syrup . . . because of course she does.

CREATOR

COLIE EHRENWORTH
Speed Rack competitor, Canada winner

1½ ounces (45 ml) reposado tequila

¾ ounce (22.5 ml) amontillado sherry

½ ounce (15 ml) Lillet Blanc

¼ ounce (7.5 ml) Maple-Sugar Syrup (recipe follows)

3 dashes Angostura bitters

HOW TO MAKE THE DRINK

Add all the ingredients to a mixing glass. Fill with ice and stir until cold. Strain into a chilled cocktail glass, and serve.

Maple-Sugar Syrup

Makes about 1¼ cups (300 ml)

½ cup (120 ml) maple syrup

½ cup (100 g) turbinado sugar

Add the maple syrup and turbinado sugar to a small saucepan with ½ cup (120 ml) water over low heat. Stir until the sugar has fully dissolved. Remove from the heat and allow the syrup to cool before pouring it into an airtight container. Store in the refrigerator for up to 4 weeks.

MODERN CLASSIC

—

A lesson in splitting bases, and the virtues of banana liqueur.

CREATOR

MS. FRANKY MARSHALL
Speed Rack competitor

¼ ounce (7.5 ml) Honey Syrup (recipe, page 260)

¼ ounce (7.5 ml) banana liqueur

¾ ounce (22.5 ml) blended scotch

1 ounce (30 ml) mezcal joven

Lemon twist, for garnish

GUILLOTINE

The story of the Guillotine is a prime example of how cocktail recipes can evolve over time. It began as a minty scotch sour, which ms. franky marshall devised while working at New York City's Holiday Cocktail Lounge. Then she added mezcal. And then at some point she nixed the lemon and mint, added banana liqueur, and started stirring rather than shaking the drink. And voilà! The Guillotine as we know it today. It's a drink that's gotten attention as mezcal has become more popular, as well as for its rare combination of scotch and mezcal, franky says. And it's a drink that offers a great deal of variability, depending on the types and brands of spirits used. She notes that choosing a blended scotch versus single malt or an Islay versus Speyside scotch will dramatically change the drink—as will the choice of mezcal. It's the intermingling of the two that makes for the biggest wild card. "There's room to be creative and tailor this drink to suit your or your guests' tastes," she says. We love that!

HOW TO MAKE THE DRINK

Add all the ingredients to a mixing glass and fill with ice. Stir until cold and strain into a snifter or rocks glass over fresh ice. Express the lemon twist over the drink, discard it, and serve.

DEALER'S
CHOICE

It's harvest season
and we want to have
our pie and drink
it, too. Give us your
greatest pie-inspired
creation using sherry,
Madeira, or port.

CREATOR

JESSI POLLAK
*Speed Rack competitor,
regional winner*

1 ounce (30 ml) applejack,
preferably Laird's Straight
Apple Brandy—Bottled in
Bond

1 ounce (30 ml) amontillado
sherry, preferably Lustau
Los Arcos

¾ ounce (22.5 ml) Apple
Cider–Demerara Syrup
(recipe follows)

1 teaspoon Pedro Ximénez
sherry, preferably Lustau
San Emilio

1 whole egg

Freshly grated cinnamon,
for garnish

À LA MODE

"This drink is meant to evoke the sensation of a first bite into warm buttery apple pie with a big scoop of cold vanilla ice cream," says Jessi Pollak. She brilliantly pulls this off with a split-base cocktail using Laird's applejack and amontillado sherry that evokes orchard fruits and flaky crust, while keeping the alcohol in check for the final drink of the night. "One of my go-to dessert cocktails is a flip because it's rich and creamy without being cloyingly sweet." Flips are made with a whole egg that's dry shaken (without ice) first and then again with added ice cubes. "It's important to seal your cocktail shaker tins well, and only shake the drink gently the first time," she explains. "Without the ice to create a vacuum seal, you run the risk of your cocktail shaker bursting open if you shake it too vigorously. Save the muscles for the ice." No PX sherry? Jessi says a splash of port would substitute nicely here.

HOW TO MAKE THE DRINK

Chill a ceramic teacup or cocktail glass. Add all the ingredients to a shaker without ice. Shake gently until well incorporated. Add ice to the shaker and shake again until frothy and chilled. Strain into the chilled teacup or cocktail glass. Grate cinnamon over the top of the drink and serve.

Apple Cider–Demerara Syrup

Makes about 1½ cups (360 ml)

1 cup (240 ml) unfiltered
apple cider

1 cup (200 g) demerara
sugar

Combine all the ingredients in a saucepan over low heat. Stir until the sugar is fully dissolved. Remove from the heat and let cool to room temperature. Store in an airtight container in the refrigerator for up to 2 months.

TALKING IN CURSIVE

"I love making culinary-based cocktails that start from creating flavors, and then using spirits to amplify those flavors," says Jess Yurko. With roots in an old-fashioned, her Talking in Cursive pulls in all sorts of warming elements to encourage extensive after-dinner lingering. The cocktail combines small measures of amaro and coffee liqueur ("additional after-dinner spirits," says Jess) and a tincture made from black peppercorns to add punctuation. The whiskey base is split with genever, "a beautiful and underutilized ingredient that brings out more of the maltiness of the whiskey," she says. Note that the tincture will need to be made a day or so ahead, so plan accordingly. Jess says tincture leftovers will be great dashed in a Gibson (page 201) or added to drinks involving mezcal.

CREATOR

JESS YURKO
Speed Rack competitor

1 ounce (30 ml) whiskey, preferably Starward Australia

½ ounce (15 ml) genever, preferably Old Duff

¼ ounce (7.5 ml) Montenegro amaro

1 teaspoon coffee liqueur, preferably Mr. Black

1 teaspoon Cane Syrup (page 260)

2 dashes Black Pepper Tincture (recipe follows)

Orange twist, for garnish

HOW TO MAKE THE DRINK

Add all the ingredients to a mixing glass filled with ice. Stir until cold and strain into a rocks glass over 1 large ice cube. Express the orange twist over the drink and place it in the glass. Serve.

Black Pepper Tincture

Makes about 1 cup (240 ml)

⅓ cup (40 g) black peppercorns

1 cup (240 ml) vodka

Lightly toast the peppercorns in a pan over low heat until they are warmed and start to crack. Remove the peppercorns from the heat and let them cool before pouring them into an airtight container. Add the vodka. Let the tincture rest for at least 24 hours at room temperature before using it. Store in an airtight container for up to a year.

We're drinking our
dessert, but we'd like
a cocktail that won't
keep us up all night.
Make us a chocolatey
nightcap—sans
coffee.

CREATOR

ANDREA
TATEOSIAN
Speed Rack competitor

1 ounce (30 ml) tawny port

¼ ounce (7.5 ml) Giffard
Banane du Brésil liqueur

1 dash Angostura bitters

1 whole egg

1½ ounces (45 ml) porter
ale

Freshly grated nutmeg and
more Angostura bitters, for
garnish

IN A STORM

After cheering on a friend who competed in the first season of Speed Rack in Washington, D.C., Andrea Tateosian was all in. "I was determined to compete for my grandmother Bea, who was a breast cancer survivor. After experiencing the enthusiasm, community, and genuine sisterhood, I was hooked." She competed in three seasons and made it to national finals twice, and she's emceed two of our regional competitions. For this Dealer's Choice, Andrea says she prefers something rich and lower in proof when it comes to nightcaps, which sent her in the direction of a flip-style drink. Flips can be made with any spirit, but sherry flips and ale flips are classic iterations. Here, she combines the two, subbing nutty, toffee-rich tawny port for the sherry, mixed with a porter-style ale, to make something that's altogether chocolatey without containing any chocolate.

HOW TO MAKE THE DRINK

Add the tawny port, banana liqueur, bitters, and egg to a cocktail shaker. Dry shake (without ice). Add ice and shake again, vigorously. Fine strain into a chilled cocktail glass. Top with the porter and 2 to 3 dashes of bitters. Grate the nutmeg over the drink, and serve.

DEALER'S CHOICE

———

Give us an espresso
martini variation
inspired by someone
close to you.

MATRIARCH MARTINI

CREATOR

HALEY TRAUB
*Speed Rack competitor,
USA national winner*

1½ ounces (45 ml) bourbon,
preferably Knob Creek

¾ ounce (22.5 ml) tart
cherry juice, store-bought

¾ ounce (22.5 ml) espresso

½ ounce (15 ml) Vanilla
Demerara Syrup (recipe
follows)

Chocolate shavings,
for garnish

Truth be told, an espresso martini (page 258) might not be the smartest before-bed drink, but Haley Traub's rendition is a favorite of ours, not only for the ingenuity in swapping bourbon for vodka and her addition of vibrant tart cherry juice, but because Haley made this drink specifically to contribute to Speed Rack's efforts in raising money for breast cancer awareness, research, and aid. Haley entered the competition and blew everyone's minds when she won the whole thing in her first year—a rarity in the competition. Her attention to detail and determination still inspire competitors today. We included this cocktail in a subscription charity box, from which we raised more than $3,000 for the Breast Cancer Emergency Fund. "I made this drink for my nana, a three-time breast cancer survivor, and my mom, and it feels pretty cool to know that a lot of folks battling breast cancer received help because of it," Haley says.

HOW TO MAKE THE DRINK

Add all the ingredients to a cocktail shaker filled with ice. Shake until cold and strain into a chilled cocktail glass. Garnish with the chocolate shavings and serve.

Vanilla Demerara Syrup

Makes about 1½ cups (360 ml)

---

1 cup (210 g) demerara
sugar

¼ teaspoon vanilla extract

Combine all the ingredients in a small saucepan with 1 cup (240 ml) water over medium-high heat. Stir until the sugar is fully dissolved and remove from the heat. Let cool to room temperature before pouring into an airtight container. Store in the refrigerator for up to 1 month.

PLAYING POTATO HEAD
HOW TO INVENT
NEW DRINKS

Anyone who grew up in the past fifty or so years probably played with a Mr. or Mrs. Potato Head at some point—those goofy oblong plastic spuds with bendy arms and a dozen or so body parts and disguises stored in a convenient back flap for playing dress-up. Believe it or not, it's this toy that spurred a philosophy for cocktail invention and it's responsible for many of the modern classics we know today. Essentially, the Potato Head ideology (adopted by many bartenders over the years, and passed on to us by Phil Ward) is this: Consider the building blocks of a classic cocktail and then begin substituting different blocks that can fill the same role. New shoes, different eyes, red lips swapped for a mustache . . . you get the idea.

This theory is at least some of the reason that we place such importance on classics in Speed Rack. In order to innovate, you have to know basic cocktail structures and templates. And once you have a grasp on these, then you can start to play around. The reason this approach so brilliantly aligns with Speed Rack's Dealer's Choice is that once you know

the vibe or mood of a drink then you can alter it in any direction. Take the old-fashioned, for example. It's a very simple drink: 2 ounces (60 ml) whiskey with a little sugar and some bitters over ice. Phil Ward used this template and swapped out the whiskey for a split base of reposado tequila (which is barrel-aged like whiskey) and mezcal, and the sugar for agave nectar (agave-based spirits meet agave-based sugar!). Ta- da! An entirely new drink was born, the Oaxaca Old-Fashioned.

The same approach can be applied to any drink, so long as you consider the function of each of the building blocks. It's how the White Negroni, for example, came to be: Keep the gin, sub the herbal, gentian-based Suze for Campari (Suze is a bitter aperitif like Campari, but it is not nearly as sweet or rich), and lightly sweet Lillet Blanc for the red sweet vermouth, and it's an entirely different take on the classic.

Swapping spirits is a very easy way to give a new face to a drink. Here are some of our favorite switches to make:

SWAPPING SPIRITS

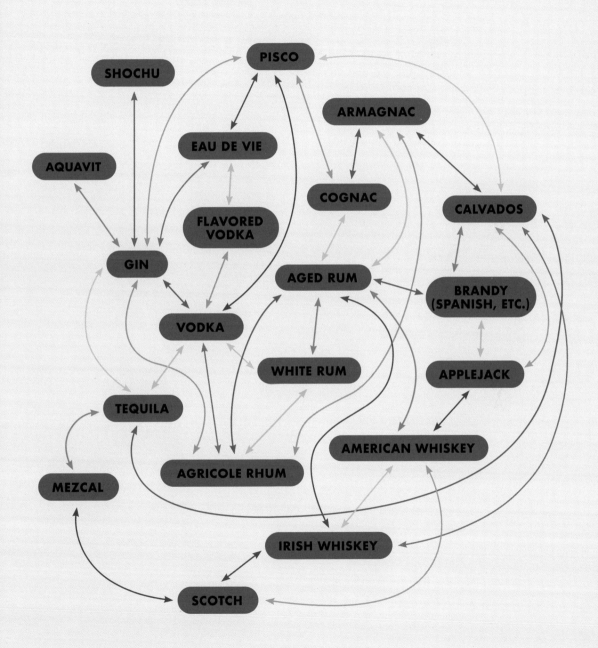

LETTER TO A YOUNG SPEED RACKER

As with so much in life, you don't win Speed Rack by accidentally signing up. You win Speed Rack by determination, hard work, practice, and sheer will to beat everyone around you. To win when you have all that at stake is going to be the best feeling ever. No competitor knows that rush better than Lacy Hawkins, who competed in five seasons before winning the whole thing.

Since claiming victory, Lacy has been contacted by numerous prospective entrants looking for advice. We thought her response, when asked about the pitfalls of Speed Rack, offered insight into not only the competition itself, but perhaps some good advice for going about life, too. She put it better than we ever could, so here's an excerpt:

Paige Rinne Unger takes flight following her Speed Rack Midwest victory in Season 3 in Kansas City.

Speed Rack isn't real.

Speed. Rack. Isn't. Real.

No matter how you compete or where you place, you're still a great bartender with an awesome job and people know you're talented. You don't need to win Speed Rack to know those things. It is hard getting up there onstage. It is hard getting past prelims! Whether you make it to stage or not, you are a better bartender because of it. The onstage experience at Speed Rack isn't like the bar you work behind. There are a million variables that just don't exist in real life—a rickety bar or a sour judge or a nicked glass or clogged speed pourer or forgotten garnish or an absentminded barback. In any bar that you work behind, you will have complete control over those things, and you can recover with a quick fix of a garnish, remaking a less-than-perfect cocktail, or just improve the experience overall with stellar hospitality. In Speed Rack, you will try to have control over those things and focus on executing your drinks with grace and style. Trust me—grace and style will go a lot further than winning.

Make friends. MAKE FRIENDS!!!

It will be so easy for you to get wrapped up in the competition and focus on winning that you'll forget why you're really there: to raise money for breast cancer research, awareness, and prevention by creating a platform where women bartenders can showcase their skills, propelling them as a talented, integral, competent, and necessary component of the beverage industry. Support the other competitors. Celebrate their victories and praise them all on high. Everyone will love you for it, and you'll look really good. Even if you can't stand someone. Celebrate their achievements. A high tide will raise all ships. You have the opportunity here to forge some very meaningful relationships or develop some awkward animosity. Don't let competitive twats bring you down.

You might lose. You might lose badly. You might lose epically. You might get embarrassed onstage. You might feel stupid or ashamed. Fuck all those feelings. And doubly fuck any judge who doesn't build you up or help you learn something. I'd love to see them try to do what you're doing. Clap your hands, smile, say thank you, and nod your head. Everyone loves to hate a sore loser—almost as much as they love to hate a happy winner.

If you make it to the stage, your first round will be the hardest. It always is. It will be like that for everyone. Your nerves will get the best of you here. Breathe deeply. Always say please and thank you. Remember to laugh and smile at the crowd. Speak clearly and remember that you've got this. You know what you're doing. You're making drinks. You do it every time you're behind the bar, and you're great at it.

Oh yeah, and have fun. It's all just a drop in the bucket :)

Lony Hawkin

THE SPEED RACK SPEC BOOK

•●●•

To be successful in Speed Rack, competitors have to know
the classics by heart. Before each competition, we send out a
spec book of the drinks that everyone will be held responsible for.
Here's a set for you at home to commit to memory.

AMERICAN WHISKEY

AMERICAN TRILOGY

1 ounce (30 ml) rye whiskey
1 ounce (30 ml) applejack brandy
1 teaspoon demerara syrup
2 dashes orange bitters

Stir, strain, serve on the rocks.

Garnish with an orange twist.

BENSONHURST

1½ ounces (45 ml) rye whiskey
¾ ounce (22.5 ml) dry vermouth
½ ounce (15 ml) Cynar
1 teaspoon maraschino liqueur

Stir, strain, serve up.

Garnish with a lemon twist.

BOULEVARDIER

1 ounce (30 ml) bourbon
1 ounce (30 ml) Campari
1 ounce (30 ml) sweet vermouth

Stir, strain, serve up or on the rocks.

Garnish with an orange twist.

FANCY FREE

2 ounces (60 ml) rye whiskey
½ ounce (15 ml) maraschino liqueur
1 dash aromatic bitters
1 dash orange bitters

Stir, strain, serve on the rocks.

Garnish with an orange twist.

LION'S TAIL

1½ ounces (45 ml) bourbon
1 ounce (30 ml) lime juice
½ ounce (15 ml) simple syrup
½ ounce (15 ml) allspice dram
2 dashes aromatic bitters

Shake, strain, serve up.

MANHATTAN

2 ounces (60 ml) bourbon or rye
1 ounce (30 ml) sweet vermouth
2 dashes aromatic bitters

Stir, strain, serve up.

Garnish with a lemon twist or cherry.

OLD-FASHIONED

2 ounces (60 ml) bourbon or rye
½ teaspoon demerara syrup
2 to 4 dashes aromatic bitters
1 to 2 dashes orange bitters (optional)

Stir, strain, serve on the rocks.

Garnish with an orange and an optional
lemon twist.

REMEMBER THE MAINE

4 to 6 dashes absinthe
2 ounces (60 ml) rye whiskey
¾ ounce (22.5 ml) sweet vermouth
½ ounce (15 ml) cherry liqueur or
cherry heering

Rinse a double rocks glass with the
absinthe and discard excess. Stir,
strain, serve in the rinsed glass.

Garnish with an orange twist or cherry.

SAZERAC

2 ounces (60 ml) rye whiskey
1 teaspoon simple syrup
3 or 4 dashes Peychaud's bitters
2 dashes Angostura bitters

Stir, strain into an absinthe-rinsed
rocks glass.

Express a lemon twist over the drink
and discard.

SCOFFLAW

1½ ounces (45 ml) rye whiskey
1 ounce (30 ml) dry vermouth
¾ ounce (22.5 ml) lemon juice
½ ounce (15 ml) grenadine
1 dash orange bitters

Shake, strain, serve up.

Garnish with an orange twist.

TORONTO

2 ounces (60 ml) rye whiskey
¼ ounce (7.5 ml) demerara syrup
¼ ounce (7.5 ml) Fernet Branca
2 dashes aromatic bitters

Stir, serve up or on the rocks.

Garnish with an orange twist.

VIEUX CARRÉ

1 ounce (30 ml) cognac
1 ounce (30 ml) rye whiskey
1 ounce (30 ml) sweet vermouth
1 teaspoon Bénédictine
1 dash aromatic bitters
1 dash Peychaud's bitters

Stir, strain, serve on 1 large ice cube.

WARD 8

2 ounces (60 ml) rye whiskey
¾ ounce (22.5 ml) lemon juice
½ ounce (15 ml) orange juice
½ ounce (15 ml) grenadine

Shake, strain, serve up.

WHISKEY SOUR

2 ounces (60 ml) bourbon
¾ ounce (22.5 ml) lemon juice
¾ ounce (22.5 ml) simple syrup
½ ounce (15 ml) egg white (optional)

Shake, strain, serve on the rocks.

BRANDY

BRANDY ALEXANDER

1 ounce (30 ml) heavy cream
1 ounce (30 ml) crème de cacao
1½ ounce (45 ml) brandy or cognac

Shake, strain, serve up.

Garnish with grated nutmeg.

BRANDY CRUSTA

2 ounces (60 ml) brandy
½ ounce (15 ml) lemon juice
¼ ounce (7.5 ml) Cointreau
¼ ounce (7.5 ml) simple syrup
1 teaspoon maraschino liqueur
1 dash aromatic bitters
Sugar rim

Shake, strain, serve up.

Garnish with an orange twist.

FRENCH 75

1½ ounces cognac or gin
½ ounce lemon juice
½ ounce simple syrup

Shake, strain into a flute, top with sparkling wine.

Garnish with a lemon twist.

SIDECAR

2 ounces (60 ml) cognac
1 ounce (30 ml) Cointreau
¾ ounce (22.5 ml) lemon juice
Sugar rim (optional)

Shake, strain, serve up.

SUFFERING BASTARD

1 ounce (30 ml) gin
1 ounce (30 ml) cognac
1 ounce (30 ml) lime juice
½ ounce (15 ml) ginger syrup
1 dash aromatic bitters

Shake, strain over ice, serve tall.

Top with soda water.

GIN

20TH CENTURY

1½ ounces (45 ml) gin
¾ ounce (22.5 ml) Cocchi Americano or Lillet Blanc
½ ounce (15 ml) crème de cacao
¾ ounce (22.5 ml) lemon juice

Shake, strain, serve up.

BIJOU

1½ ounces (45 ml) gin
1 ounce (30 ml) sweet vermouth
¾ ounce (22.5 ml) green Chartreuse
1 dash orange bitters

Stir, strain, serve up.

Garnish with an orange twist.

CLOVER CLUB

1½ ounces (45 ml) gin
½ ounce (15 ml) lemon juice
½ ounce (15 ml) raspberry syrup
½ ounce (15 ml) dry vermouth (optional)
½ ounce (15 ml) egg white

Dry shake, add ice, shake, serve up.

CORPSE REVIVER #2

¾ ounce (22.5 ml) gin
¾ ounce (22.5 ml) Cointreau
¾ ounce (22.5 ml) Cocchi Americano Bianco or Lillet Blanc
¾ ounce (22.5 ml) lemon juice
2 dashes absinthe

Shake, strain, serve up.

GIMLET

2 ounces (60 ml) gin or vodka
¾ ounce (22.5 ml) lime juice
¾ ounce (22.5 ml) simple syrup

Shake, strain, serve up or on the rocks.

HANKY PANKY

1½ ounces (45 ml) gin
1½ ounces (45 ml) sweet vermouth
¼ ounce (7.5 ml) Fernet Branca

Stir, strain, serve up.

Garnish with an orange twist.

JASMINE

2 ounces (60 ml) gin
1 ounce (30 ml) lemon juice
½ ounce (15 ml) Campari
½ ounce (15 ml) Cointreau
Simple syrup, to taste (optional)

Shake, strain, serve up.

Garnish with a lemon twist.

LAST WORD

¾ ounce (22.5 ml) gin
¾ ounce (22.5 ml) lime juice
¾ ounce (22.5 ml) green Chartreuse
¾ ounce (22.5 ml) maraschino liqueur

Shake, strain, serve up.

MARTINEZ

1½ ounces (45 ml) gin
1½ ounces (45 ml) sweet vermouth
1 teaspoon maraschino liqueur
2 dashes Angostura bitters

Stir, strain, serve up.

Garnish with an orange twist.

MARTINI

2 ounces (60 ml) gin or vodka
1 ounce (30 ml) dry vermouth
Orange bitters, to taste (optional)

Stir, strain, serve up.

Garnish with a lemon twist or an olive.

NEGRONI

1 ounce (30 ml) gin
1 ounce (30 ml) Campari
1 ounce (30 ml) sweet vermouth

Stir, strain, serve up or on the rocks.

Garnish with an orange twist.

PINK LADY

1½ ounces (45 ml) gin
½ ounce (15 ml) applejack brandy
½ ounce to ¾ ounce (15 to 22.5 ml)
lemon juice
½ ounce (15 ml) grenadine
½ ounce (15 ml) egg white

Dry shake, add ice, shake, serve up.

SATURN

1½ ounces (45 ml) gin
½ ounce (15 ml) lemon juice
½ ounce (15 ml) velvet falernum
¼ ounce (7.5 ml) orgeat
¼ ounce (7.5 ml) passion fruit liqueur

Shake, strain, serve over crushed ice.

SINGAPORE SLING

2 ounces (60 ml) gin
¾ ounce (22.5 ml) lime juice
2 ounces (60 ml) pineapple juice
¼ ounce (7.5 ml) grenadine
¼ ounce (7.5 ml) Cointreau
¼ ounce (7.5 ml) Benedictine
½ ounce (15 ml) cherry liqueur or
cherry heering
1 dash aromatic bitters

Shake, strain over ice, serve tall.

Top with soda water (optional).

VESPER

1½ ounces (45 ml) gin
¾ ounce (22.5 ml) Cocchi Americano
or Lillet
¾ ounce (22.5 ml) vodka

Stir, strain, serve up.

Garnish with a lemon twist.

IRISH WHISKEY

BRAIN-STORM COCKTAIL

2 ounces (60 ml) Irish whiskey
½ ounce (15 ml) Bénédictine
½ ounce (15 ml) dry vermouth

Stir, strain, serve up.

Garnish with an orange twist.

IRISH COCKTAIL

1½ ounces (45 ml) Irish whiskey
½ ounce (15 ml) orange Curaçao
¼ ounce (7.5 ml) maraschino liqueur
2 dashes absinthe
1 dash aromatic bitters

Stir, strain, serve up.

Garnish with an orange twist.

TIPPERARY #1

1 ounce (30 ml) Irish whiskey
1 ounce (30 ml) sweet vermouth
1 ounce (30 ml) green Chartreuse

Stir, strain, serve up.

Garnish with an orange twist or
a cherry.

RUM

AIRMAIL

1 ounce (30 ml) rum
½ ounce (15 ml) lime juice
½ ounce (15 ml) honey syrup
2½ ounces (75 ml) Champagne

Shake, strain, serve up.

DAIQUIRI

2 ounces (60 ml) rum
¾ ounce (22.5 ml) simple syrup
¾ ounce (22.5 ml) lime juice

Shake, strain, serve up.

HEMINGWAY DAIQUIRI

1½ ounces (45 ml) white rum
½ ounce (15 ml) lime juice
¾ ounce (22.5 ml) grapefruit juice
¼ ounce (7.5 ml) maraschino liqueur
¼ to ½ ounce (7.5 to 15 ml) simple
syrup, to taste (optional)

Shake, strain, serve up.

HOTEL NACIONAL

2 ounces (60 ml) dark rum
¼ ounce (7.5 ml) apricot liqueur
¾ ounce (22.5 ml) pineapple juice
½ ounce (15 ml) lime juice

Shake, strain, serve up.

Garnish with a lime wheel.

JUNGLE BIRD

1½ ounces (45 ml) dark rum
1½ ounces (45 ml) pineapple juice
¾ ounce (22.5 ml) Campari
½ ounce (15 ml) lime juice
½ ounce (15 ml) simple syrup or
demerara syrup

Shake, strain over ice, serve tall.

MAI TAI

2 ounces (60 ml) aged rum, preferably
Jamaican
¾ ounce (22.5 ml) lime juice
¼ to ½ ounce (7.5 to 15 ml) orgeat
½ ounce (15 ml) orange liqueur
Simple syrup, to taste

Shake, strain, serve over crushed ice.

Garnish with mint, a lime wheel, and an
orchid, if available.

OLD CUBAN

6 to 8 fresh mint leaves
1½ ounces (45 ml) aged rum
½ ounce (15 ml) lime juice
¾ ounce (22.5 ml) simple syrup
2 dashes aromatic bitters
Champagne, to top

Muddle the mint, add the ingredients, shake, strain, serve up.

Top with Champagne.

QUEEN'S PARK SWIZZLE

10 fresh mint leaves
2 ounces (60 ml) dark rum
¾ ounce (22.5 ml) lime juice
¾ ounce (22.5 ml) simple syrup or demerara syrup, if available
8 to 10 dashes aromatic bitters

Muddle the mint in a tall glass.

Add the ingredients and crushed ice, swizzle, top with aromatic bitters as a float.

Garnish with a mint sprig.

SCOTCH

ATHOLL BROSE

¾ ounce (22.5 ml) honey syrup
2 ounces (60 ml) single-malt scotch
4 dashes of Angostura bitters (optional)

Stir, strain, serve up.

Float a thin layer of hand-whipped cream on top.

BARBARY COAST COCKTAIL

¾ ounce (22.5 ml) blended scotch
¾ ounce (22.5 ml) gin
¾ ounce (22.5 ml) crème de cacao
¾ ounce (22.5 ml) cream

Shake, strain, serve up.

Garnish with grated nutmeg.

BLOOD AND SAND

¾ ounce (22.5 ml) blended scotch
¾ ounce (22.5 ml) orange juice
¾ ounce (22.5 ml) cherry heering
¾ ounce (22.5 ml) sweet vermouth

Shake, strain, serve up.

BOBBY BURNS

2 ounces (60 ml) blended scotch
¾ ounce (22.5 ml) sweet vermouth
¼ ounce (7.5 ml) Bénédictine

Stir, strain, serve up.

Garnish with an orange twist.

GODFATHER COCKTAIL

2 ounces (60 ml) blended scotch
1 ounce (30 ml) Amaretto

Stir, strain, serve on the rocks.

MORNING GLORY FIZZ

2 ounces (60 ml) blended scotch
¾ ounce (22.5 ml) lemon juice
¾ ounce (22.5 ml) simple syrup
½ ounce (15 ml) egg white
2 to 6 dashes absinthe

Dry shake, add ice, shake, strain, serve tall, no ice.

Top with soda water.

PENICILLIN

1½ ounces (45 ml) blended scotch
¾ ounce (22.5 ml) lemon juice
½ ounce (15 ml) ginger syrup
½ ounce (15 ml) honey syrup

Shake, strain, serve on the rocks.

Float ½ ounce (15 ml) Islay scotch on top.

ROB ROY

2 ounces (60 ml) blended scotch
1 ounce (30 ml) sweet vermouth
2 dashes aromatic bitters

Stir, strain, serve up.

Garnish with an orange twist or a cherry.

TEQUILA

EL DIABLO

2 ounces (60 ml) blanco tequila
¾ ounce (22.5 ml) lime juice
½ ounce (15 ml) ginger syrup
½ ounce (15 ml) crème de cassis

Shake, strain over ice, serve tall.

Top with soda water.

MARGARITA

2 ounces (60 ml) blanco tequila
1 ounce (30 ml) Cointreau
¾ ounce (22.5 ml) lime juice

Shake, strain, serve up or on the rocks.

MEXICAN FIRING SQUAD

2 ounces (60 ml) blanco tequila
¾ ounce (22.5 ml) lime juice
½ ounce (15 ml) grenadine
2 to 5 dashes aromatic bitters

Shake, strain, serve on the rocks.

OAXACA OLD-FASHIONED

1½ ounces (45 ml) reposado tequila
¾ ounce (22.5 ml) mezcal
1 teaspoon agave nectar
2 to 3 dashes aromatic bitters

Stir, strain, serve on the rocks.

Garnish with an orange twist (flamed optional).

PALOMA

2 ounces (60 ml) blanco tequila
¾ ounce (22.5 ml) lime juice
¾ ounce (22.5 ml) simple syrup or agave syrup
¾ ounce (22.5 ml) grapefruit juice
Salt rim (optional)

Shake, strain over ice, serve tall.

Top with soda water.

LA ROSITA

1½ ounces (45 ml) reposado tequila
½ ounce (15 ml) sweet vermouth
½ ounce (15 ml) dry vermouth
½ ounce (15 ml) Campari
1 dash aromatic bitters

Stir, strain, serve on the rocks.

Garnish with an orange twist.

VODKA

AQUEDUCT

1½ ounces (45 ml) vodka
¾ ounce (22.5 ml) Cointreau
½ ounce (15 ml) apricot liqueur
¾ ounce (22.5 ml) lime juice
Simple syrup, to taste (optional)
Shake, strain, serve up.

ESPRESSO MARTINI

1½ ounces (45 ml) vodka
1 ounce (30 ml) espresso/cold brew
¾ ounce (22.5 ml) coffee liqueur

Shake, strain, serve up.

COSMOPOLITAN

1½ ounces (45 ml) citron vodka
½ ounce (15 ml) Cointreau
½ ounce (15 ml) lime juice
1 ounce (30 ml) cranberry juice

Shake, strain, serve up.

Garnish with an orange twist (flamed optional).

MOSCOW MULE

2 ounces (60 ml) vodka
¾ ounce (22.5 ml) lime juice
¾ ounce (22.5 ml) ginger syrup

Shake, strain, serve on the rocks.

Top with soda water.

EVERYTHING ELSE

ADONIS

2 ounces (60 ml) fino sherry
1 ounce (30 ml) sweet vermouth
Orange bitters, to taste

Stir, strain, serve up.

Garnish with an orange twist.

BAMBOO

1½ ounces (45 ml) fino sherry
1½ ounces (45 ml) dry vermouth
1 teaspoon simple or cane syrup
2 dashes aromatic bitters
2 dashes orange bitters

Stir, strain, serve up.

JACK ROSE

2 ounces (60 ml) applejack brandy
¾ ounce (22.5 ml) grenadine
¾ ounce (22.5 ml) lemon juice

Shake, strain, serve up.

NAKED AND FAMOUS

¾ ounce (22.5 ml) mezcal
¾ ounce (22.5 ml) Aperol
¾ ounce (22.5 ml) yellow Chartreuse
¾ ounce (22.5 ml) lime juice

Shake, strain, serve up.

NEGRONI SBAGLIATO

1 ounce (30 ml) Campari
1 ounce (30 ml) sweet vermouth
3 to 4 ounces (90 to 120 ml) dry
sparkling wine, preferably prosecco

Add the Campari and sweet vermouth
to a wine glass with ice.

Top with sparkling wine, stir gently.

Garnish with an orange twist.

PISCO SOUR

2 ounces (60 ml) pisco
¾ ounce (22.5 ml) lime juice
¾ ounce (22.5 ml) simple syrup
½ ounce (15 ml) egg white

Dry shake, shake over ice, strain, serve up.

ROME WITH A VIEW

1 ounce (30 ml) Campari
1 ounce (30 ml) dry vermouth
1 ounce (30 ml) lime juice
¾ ounce (22.5 ml) simple syrup

Shake, strain over ice, serve tall.

Top with soda water.

SHERRY COBBLER

2 or 3 orange slices
3½ ounces (105 ml) sherry, preferably
amontillado or oloroso
½ ounce (15 ml) simple syrup

Muddle the orange slices in a shaker
tin with simple syrup. Add the sherry
and a little crushed ice. Shake, strain
into a Collins glass filled halfway with
crushed ice. Fill the glass with ice.

Garnish with ½ orange wheel, seasonal
berries, mint, and a straw.

SHERRY FLIP

2 ounces (60 ml) oloroso sherry
½ ounce (15 ml) simple syrup
1 egg

Shake without ice until frothy. Add ice
and shake until cold. Strain into a small
wine glass, and serve.

Garnish with a grating of nutmeg.

RESORCES

BARWARE AND TOOLS

COCKTAIL KINGDOM
cocktailkingdom.com

VISKI
viski.com

PANTRY ITEMS

DRIED HERBS, SALTS, AND PEPPERS (AND DRIED PURPLE CORN!)

KALUSTYAN'S
foodsofnations.com

THE SPICE HOUSE
thespicehouse.com

STARWEST BOTANICALS
starwest-botanicals.com

SOS CHEFS
sos-chefs.com

TEAS

IN PURSUIT OF TEA
inpursuitoftea.com

RARE TEA CELLAR
rareteacellar.com

MONTEREY BAY HERB CO.
herbco.com

ACID AND SPHERIFICATION POWDERS

MODERNIST PANTRY
modernistpantry.com

VERJUS

FUSION VERJUS
red and white versions available
on Amazon

WÖLFFER ESTATE WHITE AND
PETITE ROSÉ VERJUS
wolffer.com

EDIBLE GLITTER

BREW GLITTER
brewglitter.com

NON-ALCOHOLIC SPIRITS

BOISSON
boisson.co

FRUIT-BASED PUREES

THE PERFECT PURÉE OF
NAPA VALLEY
perfectpuree.com

SYRUPS

SMALL HAND FOODS
smallhandfoods.com

LIBER & CO.
liberandcompany.com

ORGEAT WORKS
orgeatworks.com

MIXERS

Specialty sodas including flavored
tonics, waters, and other cocktail
flavors like ginger beer and grapefruit
are available at many markets. These
are a few of our favorite brands:
Fever-Tree, Betty Buzz, and London
Essence.

BITTERS

There are a few widely available
brands of bitters that are absolute
must-haves for every bar: Angostura,
Peychaud's, and Regan's Orange.
We also love bitters from these
companies:

BITTERCUBE
bittercube.com

BITTERED SLING
bitteredsling.com

BITTERMENS
bittermens.com

HELLA BITTERS CO.
hellacocktail.co

SYRUPS AND SOLUTIONS

•••

AGAVE SYRUP

MAKES ABOUT 1½ CUPS (360 ML)

1 cup agave nectar

Combine the agave nectar and ½ cup water in an airtight container and stir until incorporated. Store in the refrigerator for up to 1 month.

CANE SUGAR MIX

MAKES ½ CUP (205 G)

¼ cup (100 g) superfine sugar
¼ cup (105 g) demerara sugar

Combine the sugars in a small airtight container and stir to mix well. Store in a dry place indefinitely.

CANE SYRUP

MAKES 2½ CUPS (600 ML)

2 cups (400 g) cane sugar

Combine the sugar and 1 cup (240 ml) water in a saucepan over low heat. Stir until the sugar is fully dissolved. Remove from heat and allow the syrup to cool to room temperature before pouring it into an airtight container. Store in the refrigerator for up to 1 month.

CINNAMON SYRUP

MAKES ABOUT 1½ CUPS (360 ML)

1 cup (200 ml) granulated sugar
6 or 7 (15 g) cinnamon sticks, preferably Mexican canela or India cassia bark

Combine the cinnamon and sugar with 1 cup (240 ml) water in a saucepan. Bring

to a boil then remove from heat. Allow the syrup to cool to room temperature then strain out the cinnamon and pour it into an airtight container. Store in the refrigerator for up to 1 month.

DEMERARA SYRUP

MAKES ABOUT 1½ CUPS (360 ML)

2 cups (420 ml) demerara sugar

Combine the sugar and 1 cup (240 ml) water in a saucepan over low heat. Stir until the sugar is fully dissolved. Remove from heat and allow the syrup to cool to room temperature before pouring it into an airtight container. Store in the refrigerator for up to 1 month.

GINGER SYRUP

MAKES ABOUT 1½ CUPS (360 ML)

1 cup (100 g) chopped fresh ginger
1 cup (200 g) granulated sugar

Combine the ginger, sugar, and 1 cup (240 ml) water in a saucepan and bring to a boil, stirring until the sugar is fully dissolved. Lower the heat, cover the saucepan, and let simmer for 2 minutes. Remove from heat and let sit, covered, for at least 2 hours. Strain into a bottle and store in the refrigerator for up to 2 weeks.

GRAPEFRUIT, PASSION FRUIT, ANCHO VERDE SODA WATER

MAKES 18 OUNCES (540 ML)

8 ounces (480 ml) grapefruit juice

1 ounce (60 ml) passion fruit juice
8 ounces (480 ml) soda water
1 ounce (60 ml) Ancho Reyes Verde chile liqueur

Add all the ingredients to a pitcher just before you're about to make the drink, so as to not lose the fizz in the soda water. Stir gently to incorporate.

HONEY SYRUP

MAKES ABOUT 1½ CUPS (360 ML)

1 cup (240 ml) honey

Combine the honey and ½ cup (120 ml) water in an airtight container and stir until incorporated. Store in the refrigerator for up to 1 month.

INFUSION #1

4 guajillo chiles, lightly crushed
1 ancho chile, lightly crushed
2 cascabel chiles, lightly crushed
1 bottle (750 ml) mezcal, preferably Yola

Add the crushed chiles, including the seeds, to a large food-safe container and pour the mezcal over top. Seal tight and let infuse for 4 hours, stirring and shaking occasionally. Fine strain and pour the infused mezcal through a funnel, back into its original bottle. Store in the refrigerator for up to 2 months.

INFUSION #2

1 medium (about 100 g) fresh poblano chile, charred over a flame
⅓ cup (50 g) fresh serrano chiles
⅓ cup (50 g) fresh jalapeño chiles
1 bottle (750 ml) mezcal, preferably Yola

Slice all of the chiles into wheels. Add

them (including seeds) to a large food-safe container and pour the mezcal over top. Seal tight and let infuse for 1 hour. Fine strain and pour the infused mezcal through a funnel, back into its original bottle. Store in the refrigerator for up to 2 months.

LAPSANG SOUCHONG SYRUP

MAKES ABOUT 1½ CUPS (360 ML)

¼ cup (15 g) whole-leaf lapsang souchong tea
¾ cup (150 g) granulated sugar
2 tablespoons brown sugar
1 teaspoon kosher salt

Bring 2 cups (240 ml) water to a boil in a small saucepan over high heat. Remove from heat, add the tea leaves, cover, and let steep for 15 minutes. Add the sugar to the tea and stir until completely dissolved. Let sit for 5 minutes, strain, and stir in the salt. Pour into an airtight container and allow to cool to room temperature. Store in the refrigerator for up to 1 month.

OLIVE OIL–WASHED SEEDLIP GARDEN–AMASS RIVERINE BLEND

MAKES ABOUT 12 OUNCES (360 ML)

6 ounces (180 ml) Seedlip Garden 108 distilled non-alcoholic spirit (see Resources, page 259)
6 ounces (180 ml) Amass Riverine non-alcoholic gin alternative (see Resources, page 259)
2 ounces (60 ml) high-quality extra-virgin olive oil

Pour all the ingredients into a pint-size jar. Cover and shake vigorously to combine. Let sit at room temperature to infuse for 6 hours. Transfer the jar to the freezer for 8 hours (or overnight).

The olive oil will solidify and separate. Remove from the freezer and let the jar warm up for 30 minutes. Line a fine-mesh strainer with a coffee filter, milk bag, or paper towel. Place over a second container and strain the Seedlip, discarding the solids. Repeat the process as necessary to remove any remaining oil. Keep refrigerated and use within 6 months.

NOTE If you have access to a sous vide cooker, this olive oil wash can be done much quicker. Set your machine to 140°F (60°C). Combine the ingredients in a large zip-top or reusable silicone heat-proof bag. Seal the bag, leaving the last ½ inch (1.25 cm) unsealed so air can escape. Submerge it slowly into the water, massaging the bag around the liquid to push out any air, then complete the seal. Place in the water bath and set the timer for 2 hours. Remove the bag from the water and let cool. Use the same straining methods as referenced above.

PIQUE BITTERS

MAKES 12 OUNCES (360 ML)

1 fresh habanero chile, chopped
1 fresh jalapeño, chopped
2 dried chipotle chiles, chopped
2 dried morita chiles, chopped
1 dried ancho chile, chopped
12 ounces (360 ml) overproof vodka

Add all the chopped chiles to an airtight container and pour the vodka over the top. Let infuse at room temperature for 2 weeks.

RASPBERRY SYRUP

MAKES ABOUT 1½ CUPS (360 ML)

1 cup (125 g) fresh raspberries
1 cup (200 ml) granulated sugar

Combine the berries and sugar in a jar and shake gently to coat the fruit. Let

sit for a few hours. Add the sugar and berries to a saucepan. Pour 1 cup (240 ml) water into the jar, slosh it around, and pour that water in with the berries. Over low heat, bring the mixture to a simmer. Remove from heat and cover the pan. Let sit for 1 hour, then strain the syrup through a fine-mesh strainer back into the jar. Store in the refrigerator for up to 2 weeks.

RICH SIMPLE SYRUP

MAKES ABOUT 1½ CUPS (360 ML)

2 cups (200 ml) granulated sugar

Combine the sugar and 1 cup (240 ml) water in a saucepan over low heat. Stir until the sugar is fully dissolved. Remove from the heat and allow the syrup to cool to room temperature before pouring it into an airtight container. Store in the refrigerator for up to 1 month.

ROASTED GARLIC AND PEPPER–INFUSED VODKA

First published in *Cocktail Codex* by Alex Day, Nick Fauchald, and David Kaplan (Ten Speed Press, 2018)

MAKES ABOUT 25 OUNCES (750 ML)

1 (750-ml) bottle vodka, preferably Absolut
3 or 4 cloves (12 g) roasted garlic, smashed into a paste
1 teaspoon black peppercorns, crushed

Add all the ingredients to a food-grade container and stir to combine. Cover and refrigerate for at least 12 hours. Strain through a fine-mesh sieve lined with several layers of cheesecloth, then funnel back into the vodka bottle. Store in the freezer for impromptu martinis for up to 3 months.

SALINE SOLUTION

10 grams salt
100 grams water

Stir to dissolve. Keeps indefinitely but can evaporate and become stronger.

SEASONED OLIVE BRINE

MAKES ABOUT ½ CUP (120 ML)

½ cup (120 ml) high-quality olive brine from good green olives, olives reserved
¼ teaspoon granulated sugar
2 bay leaves
3 fresh basil leaves or 1 teaspoon dried basil (can sub rosemary, oregano, or other favorite savory herb, as desired)
1 teaspoon dried green peppercorns, crushed

Combine all the ingredients in a small saucepan over low heat. Stir until the sugar dissolves and the brine is warm enough for the herbs to infuse. Cover and let infuse for 2 to 3 hours. Fine strain the brine back over the olives and refrigerate for up to 3 weeks.

SIMPLE SYRUP

MAKES ABOUT 1½ CUPS (360 ML)

1 cup (200 ml) granulated sugar

Combine the sugar and 1 cup (240 ml) water in a saucepan over low heat. Stir until the sugar is fully dissolved. Remove from heat and allow the syrup to cool to room temperature before pouring it into an airtight container. Store in the refrigerator for up to 1 month.

SPICED PINEAPPLE HONEY

MAKES ABOUT 2 CUPS (400 ML)

1 cup (240 ml) honey
8½ ounces (240 g) pineapple (flesh and skins, the bottom of the pineapple skin plus some flesh works great)
4 cardamom pods
6 cloves
2 cinnamon sticks
1 cracked tonka bean (optional)
Big pinch sea salt

Add the honey and pineapple to a saucepan and muddle to break up the fruit. Add the cardamom, cloves, cinnamon sticks, tonka bean (if using), and salt and stir. Warm over low heat but do not boil. Remove from heat when the ingredients are hot, and the pineapple is very soft. Let cool to room temperature and then fine strain into an airtight container. Store in the refrigerator for up to 1 month.

SPICY SYRUP

MAKES ABOUT 12 OUNCES (360 ML)

2 dried chiles de árbol, chopped
2 dried ancho chiles, chopped
2 dried guajillo chiles, chopped
2 cups (200 g) granulated sugar

Add the chiles and 1 cup (240 ml) water to a small saucepan over medium heat. Bring to a boil and cook for 10 minutes. Add the sugar and stir until it is fully dissolved. Turn off the heat and let the peppers infuse. Once the syrup has cooled to room temperature, strain and store in an airtight container in the fridge for up to 1 month.

UME CAVIAR

MAKES ABOUT ½ CUP (120 G)

1¼ teaspoons (3 g) sodium alginate
¾ teaspoon (2.5 g) calcium chloride
½ cup (120 ml) UME Plum liqueur

Prepare a sodium alginate solution: Combine the sodium alginate and 11 ounces (325 ml) water in a small saucepan and, using an immersion blender, blend to fully dissolve the sodium alginate into the water. (This could take 5 to 10 minutes.) Bring the solution to a boil over medium heat. Remove from the heat and allow to cool to room temperature before using. You should have about ¾ cup (180 ml).

Prepare a calcium chloride bath: Combine the calcium chloride with 17 ounces (500 ml) water, preferably distilled, in a medium bowl.

Fill a small bowl with water and set aside. Add the plum wine to the sodium alginate solution and stir to combine.

Using a pipette or dropper, gently squeeze the plum wine mixture drop by drop into the calcium chloride bath. Small spheres will form. Let them "cook" for about 1 minute, then remove them from the bath using a slotted spoon.

Place them into the bowl of clean water to rinse before serving. Store the ume caviar in an airtight container in the refrigerator for up to 5 days.

VANILLA SYRUP

MAKES ABOUT 1½ CUPS (360 ML)

1 cup (200 g) granulated sugar
1 vanilla bean

Combine the sugar and 1 cup (240 ml) water in a saucepan over low heat. Stir until the sugar is fully dissolved. Slice the vanilla bean in half lengthwise and scrape the seeds into the syrup; add the bean pod, as well. Remove from the heat and allow the syrup to cool to room temperature before fine straining it into an airtight container. Store in the refrigerator for up to 1 month.

ACKNOWLEDGMENTS

For the last thirteen years, we have been over-whelmed by the talents and contributions of our Speed Rack community. This book is a tribute to all the time, hard work, enthusiasm, and commitment to inspiring future generations of bartenders.

We also give our sincerest gratitude to the following:

To the many women who contributed recipes to this book and to the thousands more who have participated in Speed Rack around the globe. To all our volunteers, barbacks, events coordinators, and judges who donate their valuable time to make Speed Rack the incredible success that it is. To the many hosts, but especially those who came on tour, Chris Patino, Anne Louise Marquis, Robin Nance, and Vance Henderson.

To Claire Bertan-Lang, Cooper Cheatham, Becky Nadeau, and Lisa Mulligan for helping us over the years with logistics. To Lauren Mote, Evelyn Chick, Christina Veira, Vivian Pei, Holly Graham, Quynh Nguyen, Roberto Berdecia, Deliana Olmo, Amba Lamb, and Izzy Ortega, who lobbied for Speed Rack to come to their countries. To Gia Vecchio and the Foxglove team for spreading the Speed Rack word around the globe.

To Lush Life Productions for getting us going in our infancy and to Le JIT Productions for continuing to produce incredible videos that helped spread the gospel of Speed Rack far and wide. To Joe Banofato, our digital wizard taking the helm from Don Lee and John Dergon.

And to Rhachel Shaw, without whom the idea of a Speed Rack would have never come to be.

Thank you to both our Megans (Krigbaum and Rainwater) for helping us create this book from word to image, and to combine it all together. And a special shout-out to Ty Baker not only for helping creative direct this book but also for being our graphic designer since day one.

To our editor, Laura Dozier, and the whole Abrams team for working so hard to see our vision through. To our agents, Jonah Straus and David Black, for cheerleading us along the way.

In the creation of this book, we utilized several locations for photoshoots (in Chicago and NYC) and would like to thank Jason Hammel and Lula Cafe; Daniel Alonso and Coquette and Bambola; Meaghan Dorman and Dear Irving on Hudson; and Julie Reiner, Christine Williams, and Susan Fedroff and Clover Club and Leyenda.

Finally, thank you to everyone who has ever attended a Speed Rack and to you, who bought this book. You are helping us create diversity within the cocktail community and giving us the ability to continue our fight against breast cancer.

BACK THE RACK.

CONTRIBUTORS

CHAPTER 1

UNA GREEN
competitor USA season 7

NATASHA DAVID
competitor USA seasons 2 and 3

LAUREN PAYLOR O'BRIEN
competitor USA season 8

MELINA MEZA
competitor USA seasons 6–9
and 11

MISTY KALKOFEN
judge USA seasons 1–8 and
Mexico season 1

PRISCILLA LEONG
competitor Australia season 1,
national winner

SHANNON PONCHE
competitor USA season 3,
regional winner

JULIA MOMOSÉ
competitor USA seasons 5 and 6

TESS ANNE SAWYER
competitor Canada season 2,
national winner, competitor USA
seasons 4, 5, and 10

CHAPTER 2

CHRISTINA MERCADO
competitor USA seasons 6–9

JORDIE HO-SHUE
competitor USA season 8

CHRISTINA VEIRA
coordinator Canada seasons 3
and 4

KATE BOUSHEL
competitor Canada seasons 2 and
3, coordinator season 4

KATIE RENSHAW
competitor USA seasons 6 and 7,
regional winner

LYDIA MCLUEN
competitor USA seasons 6–8,
regional winner

EZRA STAR
competitor USA season 2

CARI HAH
competitor USA seasons 2–4

CHAPTER 3

MILLIE TANG
competitor Australia seasons 1
and 2, national winner

CARLEY NOEL HANSEN
competitor USA season 6

CLAIRESSA CHAPUT
competitor USA seasons 6, 8, and
10, regional winner

ANGEL TETA
competitor USA seasons 2–4,
regional winner

J'NAI ANGELLE
competitor USA season 8

KAITLYN STEWART
competitor Canada seasons 1
and 2, judge season 3

LACY HAWKINS
competitor USA seasons 1–5,
national winner

MARISELA DOBSON
competitor USA seasons 9–11

MONY BUNNI
competitor USA season 6,
national winner

SYLVI ROY
competitor USA seasons 5–9,
regional winner

CHAPTER 4

CHRISTINE WISEMAN
competitor USA seasons 3–6, regional winner, and judge season 11

EVELYN CHICK
competitor USA season 3,
competitor Canada season 1,
coordinator Canada seasons 2–4

FABIANA PINILLOS
USA competitor seasons 10 and 11,
regional winner

KELSEY RAMAGE
competitor USA season 3,
competitor UK season 3

SIAN BUCHAN
competitor UK seasons 1–4

YAEL STORMBORN
competitor USA season 1, national
winner

SARAH TROXELL
competitor USA seasons 6–9,
national winner

ERIN HAYES
competitor USA seasons 2–3

KATIE STIPE
friend of Speed Rack

KAREN TARTT
competitor USA seasons 8 and 9

**CLAUDIA CABRERA
RODRIGUEZ**
competitor Mexico season 1, judge
Mexico season 2

CHAPTER 5

BECKALY FRANKS
competitor USA seasons 1-3,
emcee Asia season 2

YANA VOLFSON
competitor USA season 1

CAER MAIKO FERGUSON
competitor USA seasons 7–9

GENEVIEVE TEMPRANO
competitor Puerto Rico Season 1,
national winnter,
competitor USA seasons 10 and 11

JESSICA GONZALEZ
friend of Speed Rack

JESSI LORRAINE
competitor USA seasons 6, 8, and
9, regional winner

MARY PALAC
competitor USA seasons 5–7,
regional winner

YOLANDA BAEZ
competitor USA season 9

GIA ST. GEORGE TERRY
competitor USA seasons 4, 5,
and 10

ELYSE BLECHMAN
competitor USA seasons 5, 6, and
10, regional winner

CHAPTER 6

ALEX JUMP
competitor USA seasons 5 and 6,
regional winner

DAPHNEE VARY DESHAIES
competitor Canada seasons 3
and 4

JULIE REINER
mentor and judge USA seasons
1–9 and 11

SUMMER LO
competitor Asia season 2, Asia
national winner

JESS POMERANTZ
competitor USA seasons 7–10,
national winner

LEANNE FAVRE
competitor USA seasons 7 and 8

MIRANDA BREEDLOVE
competitor USA seasons 5–7

SIENNA HEMBROOKE-MANN
competitor USA seasons 9 and 10

NATASHA BERMUDEZ
competitor USA seasons 7 and 9,
regional winner

ABIGAIL GULLO
competitor USA season 1

MEAGHAN DORMAN
friend of Speed Rack, judge USA
seasons 9 and 11

CHAPTER 7

ALISHA NEVERSON
competitor USA seasons 8 and 9

ANU APTE
competitor USA season 1, judge
seasons 4, 5, 7, and 8

IRENE KERN
competitor USA seasons 8 and 9

BRITTINI RAE PETERSON
competitor USA seasons 2–4,
national winner

KITTY CORBO
competitor USA seasons 7 and 8,
national winner

ERYN REECE
competitor USA season 1 and 2,
national winner

RHACHEL SHAW
competitor USA seasons 1–3

ZULCORALIS RODRÍGUEZ
competitor USA seasons 4, 5, 6,
and 8, regional winner

LEANNE FAVRE
competitor USA seasons 7 and 8

JILLIAN VOSE
competitor USA seasons 2 and 3

CHAPTER 8

BAYLEE BROOKS HOPINGS
competitor seasons 9–11, regional
winner

BRISA SANTOS C.
competitor Mexico season 2,
national winner

NATASHA MESA
competitor USA seasons 6 to 9,
regional winner

COLIE EHRENWORTH
competitor Canada season 4,
national winner

MS. FRANKY MARSHALL
competitor USA season 1, emcee
USA season 9

JENA ELLENWOOD
competitor USA season 8

JESS YURKO
competitor USA season 9

JESSI POLLAK
competitor USA seasons 7–9,
regional winner

KAPRI ROBINSON
competitor USA seasons 4, 6,
and 7

ANDREA TATEOSIAN
competitor USA seasons 4–7,
regional winner, emcee USA
seasons 7 and 9

HALEY TRAUB
competitor USA season 7,
national winner

INDEX

———•••—•

Editor: Laura Dozier
Designer: Heesang Lee
Managing Editors: Mike Richards and Logan Hill
Production Manager: Kathleen Gaffney

Library of Congress Control Number: 2023941949

ISBN: 978-1-4197-6474-5
eISBN: 978-1-64700-834-5

ABRAMS The Art of Books
195 Broadway, New York, NY 10007
abramsbooks.com